SOUTHEAST

D0990793

They Walked to Freedom

to Freedom

——— 1955-1956 ———

THE STORY OF THE MONTGOMERY BUS BOYCOTT

www.SpotlightPress.com

ISBN: 1-59670-010-6

© 2005 by The Advertiser Company, Inc. d.b.a. *Montgomery Advertiser*

All rights reserved. Except for use in a review, the reproduction or utilization of this work in any form or by any electronic, mechanical, or other means, now known or hereafter invented, including xerography, photocopying, and recording, and in any information storage and retrieval system, is forbidden without the written permission of the publisher.

Publishers: Peter L. Bannon and Joseph J. Bannon Sr.
Senior managing editor: Susan M. Moyer
Acquisitions editor: Noah Amstadter
Developmental editor: Erin Linden-Levy
Art director: K. Jeffrey Higgerson
Cover/dust jacket design: K. Jeffrey Higgerson
Interior layout: Dustin Hubbart and Heidi Norsen
Imaging: Dustin Hubbart and Heidi Norsen

Printed in the United States of America

Spotlight Press L.L.C.
804 North Neil Street
Champaign, IL 61820

Phone: 1-877-424-2665
Fax: 217-363-2073

www.SpotlightPress.com

This book is dedicated to the people of Montgomery
who took part in the "walk to freedom" and to the people
who supported them with rides, money and prayers.

Table of Contents

MONTGOMERY BUS BOYCOTT TIMELINE

May 21, 1954
Professor Jo Ann Robinson, president of the Women's Political Council made up of black Montgomerians, writes to the mayor of Montgomery to warn of the possibility of a bus boycott.

September 1, 1954
Martin Luther King Jr. becomes pastor of Dexter Avenue Baptist Church in Montgomery.

March 2, 1955
African American Claudette Colvin, 15, is arrested after allegedly violating bus segregation laws.

October 21, 1955
African American Mary Louise Smith, 18, is arrested after allegedly violating bus segregation laws.

December 1, 1955
African American Rosa Parks is arrested after allegedly violating bus segregation laws. She is charged with disorderly conduct.

December 2, 1955
Black Montgomery activists, including professor Jo Ann Robinson, attorney Fred Gray, and labor leader E.D. Nixon, begin setting the stage for a bus boycott.

December 5, 1955
Rosa Parks is convicted and fined in Montgomery city court. A one-day boycott of city buses results in about 90 percent of normal black ridership staying off buses. The Montgomery Improvement Association is formed by black leaders, who elect the Rev. Martin Luther King Jr. president. Several thousand black citizens attend the first MIA mass meeting at Holt Street Baptist Church, where they overwhelmingly support continuing the bus boycott.

December 8, 1955
The first negotiations between MIA leaders and city and bus company officials deadlock over a proposal by MIA spokesmen for a bus seating policy that is more fair to blacks but still segregated.

December 13, 1955
The MIA begins to operate a car pool system. In time, the system will grow to more than 200 private automobiles and station wagons, many of which are operated by black churches.

December 16, 1955
The vice president of the parent company of the Montgomery bus system meets with city and local bus officials and with MIA leaders. The mayor forms a biracial committee, supposedly to negotiate a compromise.

Foreword

Fifty years after the pivotal Montgomery Bus Boycott, the world reveres the legacy of Rosa Louise McCauley Parks, the quiet, unassuming seamstress who served the Montgomery branch of the NAACP as secretary and leader of a youth group. Unassuming as she was, prior to the boycott Parks had built a reputation as a defender of civil rights for black residents of Alabama and the South.

It was on December 1, 1955, that Parks, then 42 years old, took her now-famous position on a city bus in Montgomery. Weary from her workday, she boarded and sat in the front row of what was known as the colored section. As the bus traveled along Montgomery Street and white passengers filled the front section of the bus, the driver told Parks and several other blacks seated on her row to move farther back so his white passengers could sit.

Three blacks got up and walked to the rear. Tired and defiant, Parks did not budge.

The driver got off the bus, walked to a pay telephone and called police for help. The arrest of Rosa Parks opened the door to a chapter of history. Four days later, the black citizens of Montgomery, through a newly formed organization called the Montgomery Improvement Association (MIA), launched a boycott of buses that, in 381 days, led the way for the American Civil Rights Movement.

Sadly, Parks did not live to see the celebration of this anniversary. She passed away October 24, 2005, just a few weeks before the 50th anniversary celebration would begin.

The *Montgomery Advertiser* and the afternoon *Alabama Journal* chronicled the events of those 381 days. At first not even Parks understood the enormous importance of her action. Apparently, the *Advertiser* also didn't see this as the seminal event it would become, because the account of Parks's arrest appeared in a four-paragraph story on the bottom of page 9A. In fact, other black women had been arrested for violating bus segregation laws. Parks's arrest was a routine story of the day, but nothing was routine about what followed.

This story has already been told in many ways—through books, research papers, oral histories, movies, and documentaries. Grade school students across the United States study the

December 19, 1955
The biracial committee meets but cannot agree on a compromise proposal. While never disbanded, there is no record of the committee meeting again.

January 9, 1956
MIA leaders meet with city commissioners, but neither group modifies its position.

January 23, 1956
Mayor W.A. Gayle announces a tougher policy on the bus boycott, including no further negotiations with the MIA.

January 26, 1956
King is charged with speeding and jailed by Montgomery police.

January 27, 1956
After getting a series of threatening phone calls, King reports sitting at his kitchen table late into the night considering whether to abandon the leadership of the boycott. But his resolve is strengthened by a divine voice telling him to continue the fight.

January 30, 1956
At the urging of attorney Fred D. Gray, the executive board of the MIA votes to support the filing of the federal lawsuit to challenge city and state bus segregation laws. That night King's house is bombed with his wife and their infant daughter inside, but they

are not injured. An angry group of blacks, some of them armed, appears ready to react with violence, but King calms the crowd by speaking to them from his porch.

February 1, 1956
Fred D. Gray and Charles D. Langford file the *Browder v. Gayle* lawsuit on behalf of four female plaintiffs to challenge the constitutionality of city and state bus segregation laws. E.D. Nixon's home is bombed; no one is injured.

February 10, 1956
A White Citizens Council rally in Montgomery is packed with thousands who applaud city officials for fighting bus desegregation.

February 13, 1956
A Montgomery circuit judge orders a grand jury investigation into whether the bus boycott violates a state boycott conspiracy law.

February 20, 1956
Those attending a mass meeting overwhelmingly reject a bus settlement proposal by Men of Montgomery, a white businessmen's group.

nation's civil rights history, and the bus boycott figures prominently into those lessons.

They Walked to Freedom: The Story of the Montgomery Bus Boycott, 1955-1956 tells this story in great part from the perspective of the *Montgomery Advertiser* and the *Alabama Journal.* Most of the writing and research was done by Kenneth Hare, editor of the *Advertiser's* editorial page. (Hare was backed up on the writing by associate editorial page editor Jim Earnhardt.) Hare moved from his native South Carolina to Montgomery in 1979 and served the *Advertiser* first as managing editor before moving to his role on the editorial page. He has been in Montgomery long enough to fully understand the impact the bus boycott had on the city. He has served with MIA President Johnnie Carr as co-chair of One Montgomery, a group of black and white citizens who meet weekly to discuss issues of mutual interest. Hare was a natural choice to lead this book project.

This was not an easy story to tell. The fading pages of the newspapers and aging memories of surviving boycott participants made this project challenging, yet more important. Hare went

through the newspapers' microfilm and photo files to connect the events as they were reported in 1955-1956. He contacted dozens of people who were participants in the boycott or were knowledgeable about key participants. He spent many days at the Alabama Department of Archives digging up information. He took a portable scanner and laptop computer into the homes of many people in the community and made copies of their precious photographs and documents about the bus boycott. Hare gathered dozens of pictures from the *Advertiser's* dusty files and, with the help of a researcher, identified historic pages to be reproduced.

They Walked to Freedom is the *Montgomery Advertiser's* account of the Montgomery Bus Boycott. It is an effort to document the past and preserve it for the future—for the generations of young people who will study this time in history and who won't be able to meet some of the individuals whose oral history will be silenced by time.

—Wanda Lloyd, Executive Editor
Montgomery Advertiser

February 21, 1956
A Montgomery County grand jury indicts about 90 bus boycott leaders and charges them with violating a statute barring boycotts without just cause.

March 19-22, 1956
King is found guilty of violating the boycott conspiracy law. King's sentence of a $500 fine or a year in jail is delayed pending appeal. It is not until a year later that he loses his appeal and pays the fine. Other indicted MIA leaders are never tried.

March 28, 1956
A National Deliverance Day of Prayer to support the bus boycott takes place, with several cities outside the South taking part.

April 23, 1956
The U.S. Supreme Court dismisses an appeal of a July 1955 federal appeals court ruling outlawing bus segregation in South Carolina. The decision is misconstrued by many as declaring all intrastate bus segregation unconstitutional. The Montgomery bus company decides to implement a policy of desegregation.

April 24, 1956
Bus companies in more than a dozen Southern cities stop the practice of segregated seating in response to the Supreme Court decision. But the Montgomery mayor declares that city bus segregation will continue, and the police threaten to arrest bus drivers who disobey segregation laws.

May 1, 1956
Montgomery officials seek an injunction from a state judge to force the local bus company to comply with segregation laws. It is issued a week later.

May 11, 1956
A Montgomery federal court holds a hearing on the *Browder v. Gayle* lawsuit challenging bus segregation law. Claudette Colvin, Mary Louise Smith, and two other plaintiffs testify before circuit judge Richard T. Rives and district judges Frank M. Johnson Jr. and Seybourn H. Lynne.

June 5, 1956
Federal judges Rives and Johnson rule the city and state bus segregation laws are unconstitutional. Lynne dissents.

June 11, 1956
The Rev. U.J. Fields resigns as secretary of the MIA and accuses other MIA leaders of misusing funds. King returns from an out-of-state trip to address the allegations.

June 18, 1956
At an MIA mass meeting, Fields apologizes.

Acknowledgments

Without the help and encouragement of many people, this book could never have become a reality.

I would like to first thank Scott M. Brown, the publisher and president of the *Montgomery Advertiser*, who gave birth to the idea of the newspaper doing a book to commemorate the 50th anniversary of the Montgomery Bus Boycott.

A tremendous thank you also has to go to Wanda Lloyd, the executive editor of the *Advertiser*. The fact that the newspaper now has an African American as its top editor is a testament to how far it and the community have come since the boycott. Wanda not only made the resources of the newsroom available to help with this book, she personally served as an invaluable adviser, copyeditor, and proofreader. It was her project, too.

This book could never have been done without the many contributions of Jim Earnhardt, associate editorial page editor of the *Montgomery Advertiser*. Among other things, Jim, a friend of Virginia Durr late in her life, wrote the chapter on Clifford and Virginia Durr.

Other newspaper staff members who provided crucial assistance include photo editor David Bundy and assistant photo editor Karen Doerr and graphics editor Kevin Van Hyning, who helped gather and process the photos and other illustrations in the book. Researcher Hattie Robinson was a huge help in digging through the newspaper's files for background material, and Lloyce Browder and Windy Herbert provided timely typing and other clerical assistance. Tina McManama, marketing development director for the *Montgomery Advertiser*, provided insightful advice and sharp eyes for proofreading.

I am especially grateful for all of the people in the community who provided interviews, helped gather photos and other information, and made many helpful suggestions. These include Ray White, Troy University's vice chancellor for its Montgomery campus, and Georgette Norman, director of Troy's Rosa Parks Library and Museum. Troy University's museum dedicated to Rosa Parks has helped to protect the documents of the Civil Rights Era in Montgomery, and is a

June 19, 1956
Federal judges in Montgomery issue an injunction against segregation on Montgomery buses, but suspend its enforcement pending an appeal to the U.S. Supreme Court.

August 25, 1956
The home of Lutheran minister Robert Graetz, a white member of the MIA board, is bombed. No one is injured.

November 13, 1956
With no dissent, the U.S. Supreme Court upholds the Montgomery federal court's *Browder v. Gayle* decision striking down Alabama's bus segregation laws.

November 14, 1956
Those attending an MIA mass meeting unanimously vote to end the bus boycott when the U.S. Supreme Court decision is implemented.

December 17, 1956
The U.S. Supreme Court rejects the Montgomery City Commission's appeal of the *Browder v. Gayle* decision.

December 20, 1956
The Supreme Court's *Browder* ruling takes effect. Those attending mass meetings of the MIA again vote to end the bus boycott.

December 21, 1956
Black citizens desegregate Montgomery buses after the 13-month boycott. The bus company resumes full service.

December 23, 1956
Someone shoots into King's home.

December 24, 1956
Five white men attack a 15-year-old black girl at a Montgomery bus stop.

December 26, 1956
Rosa Jordan, a black woman, is shot in both legs while riding a Montgomery bus.

December 31, 1956
A sniper fires on another city bus.

January 10, 1957
Four churches and two homes are bombed: Bell Street Baptist, Hutchinson Street Baptist, First Baptist and Mount Olive Baptist, plus the homes of the Revs. Robert Graetz and Ralph Abernathy. An unexploded bomb is found on the porch of King's parsonage.

must stop for visitors to Montgomery who are interested in the Civil Rights Movement.

Others who helped include Ken Tilley with the Alabama Department of Archives and History; Janice Franklin, director of the Alabama State University Library, which houses the papers of the late E.D. Nixon; Thomas McPherson, a member of the Dexter Avenue King Memorial Baptist Church who works with the King parsonage; and Ann Durr Lyon, daughter of the late Clifford and Virginia Durr.

Special thanks have to go to four key participants in the Montgomery Bus Boycott, who gave generously of their time in providing interviews and background for the book. They are attorney Fred Gray, Mrs. Johnnie Carr, and the Rev. Robert Graetz and his wife, Jeannie. While I have known and worked on community projects with Mrs. Carr for years, it was well worth the effort that went into writing this book just to get to know the others better.

Erin Linden-Levy with Spotlight Press provided crucial encouragement during the book's production. We thank her for her professionalism, her patience and her gentle prodding.

I also would be remiss if I did not thank my wife, Julie, a former reporter who not only provided advice and guidance, but who also showed extreme patience with the time dedicated to this project.

Finally, the biggest thank you has to go to those thousands of unnamed and largely unrecognized men and women who, in 1955 and 1956, showed tremendous courage and personal sacrifice to make the Montgomery Bus Boycott a success. They truly walked to freedom, and in doing so helped to make this nation a better place.

Kenneth M. Hare

Hare is editorial page editor of the Montgomery Advertiser.

They Walked to Freedom

to Walked Freedom

—————— 1955-1956 ——————

THE STORY OF THE MONTGOMERY BUS BOYCOTT

Before
Rosa Parks

When Rosa Parks refused to give up her bus seat so that a white man could sit, on the afternoon of December 1, 1955, it set into motion one of the pivotal civil rights movements in the history of the United States—the Montgomery Bus Boycott.

Now, five decades later, every fifth-grade student in America studies the basics of the story: how the courage of a 42-year-old seamstress started the Montgomery Bus Boycott; how that movement propelled the Rev. Martin Luther King Jr. into national prominence; and how it set the stage for nonviolent protest as the primary means of promoting racial equality in the United States.

But at the time, few people, even Parks, understood the significance of her action.

Consider how the *Montgomery Advertiser* played the story, at the bottom of page 9A with a one-column headline that read, "Negro Jailed Here For 'Overlooking' Bus Segregation." The four-paragraph story gave the simplest outline of what happened, with no hint of the impact that was to come.

In retrospect, local journalists can be forgiven for missing the significance of the arrest of Mrs. Parks. After all, other black women had been arrested in similar circumstances, including two earlier that year, with little impact up to that point.

But a series of circumstances had been building for months that made the arrest of Mrs. Parks into far more than just another footnote in the history of black-white relations in the United States.

Montgomery, Alabama, was founded in 1819 with the merger of two existing towns and was designated as the capital of the state in 1847. Its location on the northern edge of the Black Belt, named for its fertile, dark soil, made the city a hub for the agricultural commerce of pre-Civil War plantations and the farms that replaced them after the war. Montgomery was also a natural destination for black Alabamians migrating from those farms into the cities after World War I and during the Great Depression.

Montgomery also was the first Capital of the Confederacy briefly before the seat of government was moved to Richmond, Virginia. The telegraph order to fire on Fort Sumter was sent from a building on Dexter Avenue just four blocks from the church where a young Martin Luther King Jr. would later be named pastor.

Participants in the historic Selma-to-Montgomery Voting Rights March in 1965 marched by the building where the telegram was sent and ended their march at the State Capitol where Jefferson Davis was sworn in as president of the Confederacy.

Today the city of Montgomery, with little outward acknowledgment of the irony involved, accurately dubs itself both the Cradle of the Confederacy and the Birthplace of the Civil Rights Movement.

The pieces of the puzzle that became the bus boycott started being put into place long before 1955.

Civil rights activism by black citizens started decades before, centering largely on voter registration efforts. One major player in this effort, and later an organizer of the boycott, was undertaker Rufus Lewis, a former football coach. Lewis also ran a black social club, where he would allow no members who were not registered voters.

An even more ardent crusader for equal rights issues in Montgomery was E.D. Nixon, a Pullman train porter who led the state chapter of the Brotherhood of Sleeping Car Porters. He organized the Montgomery Voters League in 1943 and served as president of both the state and local chapters of the NAACP. In the 1950s, it was Nixon to whom most blacks in trouble in Montgomery turned for help in dealing with the white system.

A key piece of the puzzle was the creation in 1949 of the Women's Political Council under the leadership of Mary Fair Burks, who chaired the English Department at historically black Alabama State University in Montgomery. The WPC became an effective lobbying force in city politics and government.

During the early 1950s, Jo Ann Robinson, an English professor at ASU, became president of the WPC, and she made one of the core causes of the WPC the improvement of the treatment of blacks by the city's bus system.

Shortly after coming to Montgomery in 1949, Robinson boarded a city bus. Northern-born, she was not familiar with the seating policy on Montgomery buses, so she took a seat in

Negro Jailed Here For 'Overlooking' Bus Segregation

A Montgomery Negro woman was arrested by city police last night for ignoring a bus driver who directed her to sit in the rear of the bus.

The woman, Rosa Parks, 634 Cleveland Ave., was later released under $100 bond.

Bus operator J. F. Blake, 27 N. Lewis St., in notifying police, said a Negro woman sitting in the section reserved for whites refused to move to the Negro section.

When Officers F. B. Day and D. W. Mixon arrived where the bus was halted on Montgomery street, they confirmed the driver's report.

Blake signed the warrant for her arrest under a section of the City Code that gives police powers to bus drivers in the enforcement of segregation aboard buses.

The *Montgomery Advertiser* ran this small story on page 9A after Rosa Parks was arrested on December 1, 1955.

the almost-empty front of the bus. Robinson was terrified when the driver yelled at her, and fearing he was going to hit her, she fled the bus. The incident made her vow to do something to improve the bus situation for blacks.

The Montgomery buses had long been a point of contention for blacks, who considered the separate seating system demeaning. A special irritant was the requirement that black riders first board a bus through the front door, pay their fare, then exit and re-enter the bus through the back door. Occasionally drivers would pull away before the would-be rider had a chance to reboard the bus.

In her memoir, Robinson recalled several confrontations between black riders and the bus system leading up to 1955. She wrote that Mrs. Geneva Johnson was fined 10 years before when she was arrested for "talking back" to a driver who scolded her for not having correct change. She also reported that Mrs. Viola White and Miss Katie Wingfield of Montgomery also were arrested and fined for the offense of sitting in front seats reserved for whites, as were two children who were visiting from New Jersey and not accustomed to segregated seating.

But one pre-Rosa Parks incident in particular served as a key piece of the puzzle that set the stage for what came later: the arrest on March 2, 1955, of a 15-year-old girl, Claudette Colvin, for refusing to give up her seat to a white person.

Colvin, as she later recalled, was well within her legal rights not to give up her seat. She was not in the front seats reserved for whites, and there was no other place for her to sit. Blacks sitting behind the white reserved section in a bus were only required to give up their seats to whites if there was another seat available farther back.

Young attorney Fred Gray, a key figure in the later boycott and lawsuit to overturn the segregation of city buses, represented Colvin.

"Claudette had more courage, in my opinion, than any of the persons involved in the movement," Gray said of his young client. "She had no idea when she left home that morning that she was going to be arrested."

Gray said Colvin made her stand, despite not knowing how she would get out of jail or what eventually would happen to her.

The black community rallied around Colvin, attempting to exonerate her through the justice system. But authorities treated her harshly, charging her with disorderly conduct and resisting arrest in addition to violating the state's segregation law. Her conviction caused the young straight-A student to burst into tears.

Gray would later say, "Claudette gave to all of us the moral courage to do what we later did."

Soon thereafter another young woman also was arrested for refusing to give up her seat to a white person. But the arrest of Mary Louise Smith, 18, on October 1, 1955, did not become generally known until several weeks afterward, so it did not play a significant role in setting the stage for the boycott. But it was a factor in a later lawsuit against the bus system.

Through the Colvin case, the black community saw that working through the white-dominated local justice system would not be enough. All but one piece of the puzzle was in place, and it came on the afternoon of December 1, 1955.

> ## "[Claudette Colvin] had no idea when she left home that morning that she was going to be arrested."
> ### —FRED GRAY

E.D. Nixon accompanies Rosa Parks to the court-house for her trial. *AP/WWP*

A PROFILE: E.D. Nixon

E.D. Nixon, and not Martin Luther King Jr., almost led the Montgomery Bus Boycott.

In fact, a case can be made that if fairness had prevailed during the four days between the arrest of Rosa Parks and the decision to make the boycott permanent, the civil rights activist who had worked for decades for better treatment for blacks would have been the natural choice over a young minister with almost no civil rights background at the time. But other factors, including the desire to find a spokesman for the boycott who would avoid the divisions among local black leaders at the time, led to the choice of King instead of Nixon.

When blacks were harassed by Montgomery's white establishment during the years leading up to the boycott, Nixon was the man toward whom they usually turned. He had served as state president of the NAACP and was a longtime president of the local chapter of the influential International Brotherhood of Sleeping Car Porters. He wielded power in black communities and held the ear of white leaders at the state and local levels. His job as a Pullman car porter made him well traveled for a working-class black man at that time. Although he was not formally educated, blacks and whites with whom he had contact in Montgomery viewed him as a man with both a sharp intellect and a good deal of wisdom.

The Rev. Ralph D. Abernathy told the *Montgomery Advertiser* several years later that prior to the boycott, he and King had informally discussed who should lead a local civil rights movement if one could be mounted.

"I had always argued that [E.D.] Nixon should be the president," Abernathy said. "He's a brave, courageous man who's not afraid to stand up for his convictions."

Nixon, one of eight children, was born July 23, 1899. His father was a tenant farmer and a preacher, his mother a cook and a maid. After his mother died when he was 10, he was raised by his aunt in a rural area near Montgomery. He only completed the first few grades of elementary school, and he left home to support himself at 14.

After a series of jobs, he became a baggage handler at the Montgomery train station. That led to his work as a Pullman porter, where he became a follower of A. Philip Randolph, the organizer of the Brotherhood of Sleeping Car Porters.

E.D. Nixon was among the 89 boycott leaders arrested in February 1956. *Montgomery County Archives*

Randolph's teachings greatly influenced Nixon, helping to form the belief system that led him to struggle for the rights of blacks in later years. In 1938, Nixon started and served as the president of a local chapter of the organization for more than two decades. Once the union gained strength, his stature in it gave him an independence from local officials that allowed him to stand up for the rights of Montgomery blacks.

That is a role that, starting in the 1930s, Nixon increasingly took on. He helped to organize groups that sought more equitable treatment for blacks in government jobs and in relief efforts. He also worked diligently to help register blacks to vote.

Author John White, in his essay "E.D. Nixon and the White Supremacists" (in the collection *Before Brown: Civil Rights and the White Backlash in the Modern South*) notes one interesting manifestation of Nixon's aggressive defense of blacks who were being wronged by the white establishment: his work as an amateur, but often effective, "sleuth."

White quotes an assistant national director of NAACP branches who visited Montgomery to look into allegations by Nixon of poor leadership in the local branch. While siding with Nixon and noting that he would be the natural leader of the organization, the national official cautioned: "The big trouble with Nixon [as an NAACP official] is that he fancies himself as an amateur detective. While I was there he was deeply involved in a criminal investigation, and his talk was mostly of other cases in which he played the role of sleuth."

White wrote that "Nixon personally investigated many cases involving police brutality; rapes of African-American women, rapes and murders. In one instance he managed to persuade Alabama governor Chauncey Sparks to commute the death sentences of three African-American men found guilty of raping a white woman to life imprisonment."

Montgomery Bus Boycott attorney Fred Gray, who credited Nixon as a major factor in encouraging him to attend law school, said Nixon always thought "everybody is somebody."

"It reminds me of what one of the husbands of a plaintiff in the [boycott] lawsuit told me. He said, 'I am not highly educated, but I'm highly elevated.' That's the kind of person Nixon was. He thought everybody had basic rights, and they should be treated right," Gray said.

Of Nixon's role in the boycott, Gray said: "He laid the foundation for what took place. If there had been no E.D. Nixon to get into the ruts and gullies and try to do something when it was very unpopular, things would not have been accomplished."

During the years before his death in 1987, Nixon became increasingly embittered—with some justification—over what he saw as a lack of recognition at the national level of his role in the Montgomery Bus Boycott. He also was critical of the Rev. Martin Luther King Jr.'s leadership and what he saw as King's snubbing of him.

But by far most Montgomery blacks who participated in the boycott understood the importance of Nixon's role and openly gave him credit. Mrs. Johnnie Carr, who led the Montgomery Improvement Association for decades following the bus boycott, said of the man she called "Nick": "He was a fighter. He would go up against anything that was wrong to try to make it right. He was against a lot of things, but he went about it in such a way that you had to respect him and listen to what he said."

Rosa Parks and E.D. Nixon (left) arrive in court in March 1956. *AP/WWP*

The Arrest

When Rosa Parks left her job as a seamstress to catch a bus on the afternoon of December 1, 1955, she didn't set out to make history. She was tired and just wanted to go home.

But when the bus driver asked her to give up her seat so that a white man could sit there, she couldn't bring herself to do it.

"I didn't get on the bus with the intention of being arrested," she often said later. "I got on the bus with the intention of going home."

Neither did she sit in the section at the front of the bus reserved for white passengers, although the story is sometimes told that way. She said she took the only remaining seat in the section for blacks.

"The back of the bus was all filled up with black people already," she said.

But the driver noted that there were two or three white men standing, so he asked that four black passengers, including Parks, give up their seats so the whites could sit.

(Interestingly, the driver violated the bus regulations when he did so, since blacks seated in the section set aside for them did not have to relinquish their seats to whites unless there were other seats available.)

Rosa Parks is fingerprinted after her arrest on December 1, 1955. *AP/WWP*

E.D. Nixon (center) and attorney Fred Gray (right) appear in court with Rosa Parks. *AP/WWP*

"The time had just come when I had been pushed as far as I could stand to be pushed, I suppose."

—ROSA PARKS

The other passengers reluctantly stood and moved back, but Rosa Parks did not. While she had no way of knowing her action would set in motion the pivotal Montgomery Bus Boycott, she knew one thing. Her own personal bus boycott began that day.

"I knew that as far as I was concerned, I would never ride on a segregated bus again."

While her stand was on the one hand a spur-of-the-moment decision, it still was not done lightly. Although Rosa Parks was a quiet and seemingly unassuming woman, she had been involved in civil rights activism for several years, although in a much less central role than the one she was about to assume. In a sense, her whole life had prepared her for this moment.

As a young girl, she had seen the results of segregation growing up in the small rural community of Pine Level, Alabama. There she attended elementary school in a shack with only a wood stove for heat, while her white counterparts attended a newer school with central heat. When she moved up to a private school for African-American girls in Montgomery, she saw her white teachers snubbed in the white community because they taught at the school. As an adult, she was active in voter registration drives and the NAACP, serving as president of the NAACP Youth Council. She also acted as secretary to E.D. Nixon, who for years prior to the bus boycott was the leading civil rights activist in Montgomery and one of the leaders in the state. She had

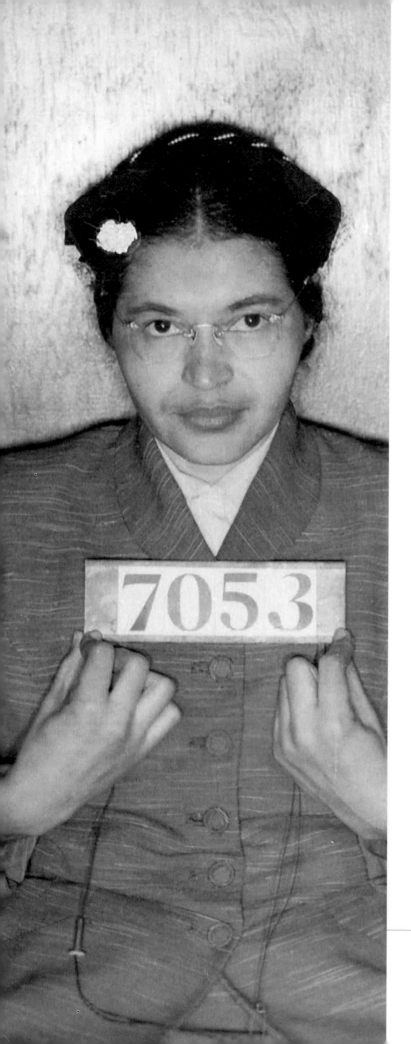

attended a training workshop for activists at the Highlander Folk School in Tennessee, where she had been stirred by messages of equality.

Earlier on the day of her arrest, she had lunched in the office of young black attorney Fred Gray, who later led the legal team that challenged bus-segregation policies. Gray recalls in his memoir, *Bus Ride to Justice*, that in similar shared lunches in his office, he and Parks had discussed the earlier arrest of 15-year-old Claudette Colvin for refusing to give up her bus seat and even the possibility of a boycott. So while her refusal to move to the back of the bus was not premeditated, it also should not have been a surprise to those who knew Rosa Parks best.

In 1956 she told radio interviewer Sidney Rogers, "The time had just come when I had been pushed as far as I could stand to be pushed, I suppose."

So when ordered by the bus driver to give up her seat, she did not move. And she still did not move when the driver threatened to have her arrested.

She later told the Associated Press: "I told him to go on and have me arrested. I wasn't frightened. I felt somewhat annoyed at being inconvenienced by not being able to get home as I had planned."

Parks was booked at the Montgomery police station. She was quickly bailed out of the city jail by her friend E.D. Nixon and white attorney Clifford Durr, a former high-ranking official in the Roosevelt Administration. They were accompanied by Durr's wife, Virginia, a friend of Parks who was active in anti-segregation efforts in the South and a sister-in-law of Supreme Court Justice Hugo Black.

Parks, Nixon, and the Durrs returned to her home, where Nixon overcame her husband's objections and persuaded Parks to allow her arrest to be used as the basis of a challenge to bus segregation laws.

Rosa Parks was arrested the second time with her fellow boycott leaders in February 1956.
Montgomery County Archives

> ## "I was fortunate God provided me with the strength I needed at the precise time conditions were ripe for change. I am thankful to him every day that he gave me the strength not to move."
>
> ### –ROSA PARKS

Parks, who was always modest about her role in the Civil Rights Movement, later gave credit to a higher power for her decision not to give up her seat, saying that as she sat there she recalled Bible lessons that taught that people should stand up for their rights as the children of Israel stood up to Pharaoh. She was quoted in the *Montgomery Advertiser* years later as saying: "I was fortunate God provided me with the strength I needed at the precise time conditions were ripe for change. I am thankful to him every day that he gave me the strength not to move."

Johnnie Carr, a longtime friend of Rosa Parks who played a key role in the desegregation of Montgomery public schools several years after the bus boycott, simply describes what happened on December 1: "A woman sat down and the world turned around."

It did not take long for that movement to begin.

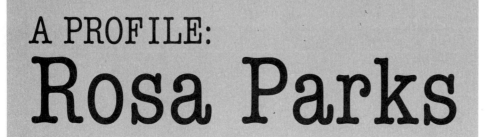

A PROFILE:
Rosa Parks

The story of Rosa McCauley Parks and her refusal to give up her bus seat so a white man could sit is usually told as a straightforward tale of a quiet and unassuming seamstress who, in a moment of spontaneous courage, helped to change American society forever.

That's a story supported by the accounts of the day, and one that is gripping and moving, partially because of its simplicity. But because of the one-dimensional impression it leaves of Rosa Parks, it is far from being the full story. It is an account that ironically has both served to elevate Parks to the level of national icon while undervaluing her long-held and strong commitment to civil rights and racial equality.

Parks was in fact quiet, and she was unassuming. But underneath that demeanor was a woman who had a history of fighting for civil rights for more than two decades before her refusal to give up her bus seat that day in 1955.

Rosa Parks stands in front of the state Capitol in Montgomery 40 years after the bus boycott.
AP/WWP

Rosa Parks receives a kiss from her mother, Leona McCauley. *Detroit News file photo*

There were many forces in Rosa Parks's early life that helped to forge her brand of quiet activism.

She had worked for years with the NAACP, serving as secretary of the Montgomery branch and as president of a youth group. She had been a secretary and aide to E.D. Nixon, who had built a reputation for decades prior to the bus boycott as one of the more outspoken defenders of black civil rights in Alabama and the South. As far back as the early 1930s, she and her husband had worked to save the Scottsboro Boys, eight black youths sentenced to death after being falsely accused of rape. She had attended the Highlander Folk School in Tennessee, which was then seen by the white establishment as a champion of radical social change.

Parks was born Rosa Louise McCauley on February 4, 1913, in Tuskegee, Alabama. Her parents were James and Leona McCauley. Her mother was a schoolteacher. Her father was an itinerant stonemason and carpenter, a respected profession for a black man of his day, but one that kept him away from home much of the time. During his travels, he left his wife and daughter with his family in an overcrowded home in Abbeville, Alabama. When the child's mother tired of this and moved back to her family in the tiny farming community of Pine Level, south of Montgomery, James McCauley essentially abandoned his wife and daughter.

Rosa McCauley's childhood in Pine Level revolved around the Mount Zion AME Church where her uncle was the pastor. Her strong faith was built in the church, but so was something else—a sense of racial pride. The African Methodist Episcopal Church had for generations been a strong advocate for black equality, something of which Parks spoke proudly later in life.

She also was strongly influenced by her grandparents, especially her grandfather. He responded to the ongoing threat of the Ku Klux Klan by keeping a loaded double-barreled shotgun nearby. While the very real possibility of Klan violence never materialized for her or her immediate family, her grandfather's defiant attitude helped mold her thinking.

When she turned 11, Rosa McCauley's horizons widened when she was sent to the Montgomery Industrial School for Girls. The school, organized by two white women, had an all-black student body and an all-white teaching staff. At the school, Parks learned self-respect and "to believe we could do what we wanted in life." She also learned from the teachers and especially one of the founders, Miss Alice L. White, that not all white people were bigots.

It was at Mrs. White's school that Parks met Johnnie Carr, and the two women started a friendship that would last a lifetime. Carr later invited Parks to join the NAACP. Several years after the Montgomery Bus Boycott, Carr and her family successfully challenged Montgomery's school desegregation in court. Carr was later president of the Montgomery Improvement Association for more than three decades.

Carr said of her friend's childhood: "I was noisy and talkative, but she was very quiet and always stayed out of trouble. But whatever she did, she always put herself completely into it. She was so quiet you never would have believed she would get to the point of being arrested."

(continued on page 22)

"I was noisy and talkative, but she was very quiet and always stayed out of trouble. But whatever she did, she always put herself completely into it. She was so quiet you never would have believed she would get to the point of being arrested."

–JOHNNIE CARR

Johnnie Carr, a lifelong friend of Rosa Parks, was a key figure in the bus boycott and has served as president of the Montgomery Improvement Association since 1967. *David Bundy/Advertiser*

Under constant pressure from some in the white community, the Industrial School closed when Parks was in the eighth grade. She then attended the laboratory school at Alabama State Teachers College for Negroes. She wanted to be a teacher but had to drop out of school to care for her ailing mother. (She later received her high school diploma.) She worked as a housekeeper for white families and took in sewing on the side.

When she was 18, she fell in love with barber Raymond Parks, who was one of the charter members of the Montgomery Chapter of the NAACP. They married in December 1932.

According to her biography (*Rosa Parks*, by Douglas Brinkley), Raymond Parks was secretly a member of a national organization trying to win justice for the falsely accused Scottsboro Boys. Early in their marriage, the young Rosa Parks saw her home used for clandestine strategy meetings.

Rosa Parks worked as a seamstress before and during the bus boycott, but was unable to find work after. *Don Cravens/Time Life Pictures/Getty Images*

During part of World War II, Rosa Parks worked at Maxwell Field (now Maxwell Air Force Base) in Montgomery, which was racially desegregated. She later noted how her indignation at having to ride on segregated buses once she left the military base was fueled by the contrast with being able to use integrated transportation while on the base.

After the Montgomery Bus Boycott ended in 1956, life in Montgomery changed dramatically for Rosa Parks, and not all of it for the better. While she was one of the nation's most honored women, she often met resentment on the part of blacks in Montgomery, some of whom were jealous of her fame. Even after the boycott ended, she and her husband continued to receive death threats, and her notoriety made it impossible for either of them to find work. So in 1957, she and Raymond Parks gave in to the urgings of her brother Sylvester and moved to Detroit, Michigan.

After moving to Detroit, Michigan, Rosa Parks (center) remained active in the civil rights movement.
Detroit News file photo

Coretta Scott King (left) kisses Rosa Parks after presenting her with the Martin Luther King Jr. Nonviolent Peace Prize in 1980. *AP/WWP*

But Parks did not give up her work for civil rights. On several occasions she joined her old friend, the Rev. Martin Luther King Jr., to lend support for his efforts, including the March on Washington in 1963. She worked in the campaign of a little-known congressional hopeful, John Conyers, and when he won a surprise victory joined his Detroit staff in 1965. She continued to work for him until she retired in 1988. Conyers often joked that he had more people visit his office to meet his staff assistant than to meet him.

In 1987, Parks and her friend Elaine Eason Steele created the Rosa and Raymond Parks Institute for Self-Development.

Parks received many honors and awards. She was inducted into the Michigan Women's Hall of Fame in 1983 and into the National Women's Hall of Fame in 1993. She was presented the Medal of Freedom Award by President Clinton in 1996 and the Congressional Gold Medal in 1999. The Southern Christian Leadership Council established an annual Rosa Parks Freedom Award in her honor. In November 2001, Troy State University in Montgomery dedicated the Rosa Parks Library and Museum in honor of her legacy.

In the last few years of her life, Parks suffered from dementia and made few public appearances. She died quietly in her apartment in Detroit on October 24, 2005, just a few weeks before the 50th anniversary of her courageous refusal to give up her seat on a bus. She was 92. Among many tributes, the mayors of Montgomery and Detroit honored the civil rights pioneer by placing black ribbons on the first seats of their city buses, reserving those seats as a fitting tribute to her legacy. The nation's leading political, religious and civil rights figures praised her life and contributions, including U.S. Congressman John Conyers (D-Mich.), for whom she worked for many years: "I remember her as an almost saint-like person. And I use that term with care. She was very humble, she was soft-spoken, but inside she had a determination that was quite fierce."

Rosa Parks attends the groundbreaking ceremony of the Rosa Parks Library and Museum in 1998.
Mickey Welsh/Advertiser

The Montgomery Improvement Association

The arrest of Rosa Parks was a small breach in a dam of pent-up frustration and anger among the black citizens of Montgomery. The leak that started with her arrest on December 1 had become a torrent by December 5, when the Montgomery Improvement Association was born and the Montgomery Bus Boycott became a reality.

Many of the most significant decisions influencing not only the boycott, but also the entire civil rights movement of the 1950s and 1960s, were made behind the scenes between the time of Parks's arrest late that Thursday and the historic flood of events the following Monday.

After leaving the Parks home, E.D. Nixon talked on the telephone with Alabama State College professor Jo Ann Robinson, who had conferred with attorney Fred Gray. They all were in agreement that a long-term legal challenge of bus segregation should be underscored by a one-day boycott of the bus system. That evening Nixon and Robinson went about setting the boycott into motion, but in ways that reflected their differing personalities.

Nixon spent the late evening talking on the telephone and drawing up a list of names of people whose support he felt was essential, including many of the more prominent black leaders of Montgomery.

But Robinson, who had been pushing for a bus boycott for months, saw an opportunity and took it. Gray, who had been out of town during the afternoon, phoned her late that evening. The two discussed the possibility of a boycott, and Robinson immediately set to work. In her memoir, Robinson recalls some notes she made that evening: "The Women's Political Council will not wait for Mrs. Parks's consent to call for a boycott of city buses. On Friday, December 2, 1955, the women of Montgomery will call for a boycott to take place on Monday, December 5."

Jo Ann Robinson, a professor at what is now Alabama State University, issued the first call for a bus boycott and was among the 89 boycott leaders indicted in February 1956. *Montgomery County Archives*

By about midnight, Robinson had written the text of a flier calling for a boycott. She called a colleague at Alabama State, the head of the business department, who agreed to let her use the department's mimeograph machine to print the flier. With his help and the aid of two of her students, Robinson spent the early morning hours of December 2 duplicating, cutting, and bundling the flier. They finished about 4 a.m., only about 10 hours after the arrest of Parks.

The flier read:

"Another Negro woman has been arrested and thrown in jail because she refused to get up out of her seat on the bus for a white person to sit down. It is the second time since the Claudette Colvin case that a Negro woman has been arrested for the same thing. This has to be stopped. Negroes have rights, too, for if Negroes did not ride the buses, they could not operate. Three-fourths of the riders are Negroes, yet we are arrested, or have to stand over empty seats. If we do not do something to stop these arrests, they will continue. The next time it may be you, or your daughter, or mother.

members of the WPC to discuss the distribution, helped by the fact that the organization had pre-planned for such a possibility. During the later morning and early afternoon, bundles of leaflets were dropped off at black schools, businesses, barber shops—anywhere blacks were likely to congregate.

Robinson and the WPC had made a boycott of the Montgomery bus system—a one-day version—a fait accompli. More conservative black leaders had little recourse but to go along with it.

Meanwhile that Friday morning, Nixon had set about calling to recruit those whose leadership he felt was essential. Among them were the Rev. Ralph Abernathy and the Rev. H.H. Hubbard, who quickly came aboard. But when he called the Rev. Martin Luther King Jr., there was some hesitation. King asked for time to mull the proposal and to be called back later. Later that day, after momentum for the protest had built, he agreed to join in. As Nixon telephoned leaders, they in turn contacted others. A meeting was arranged to be held at King's church.

"On Friday, December 2, 1955, the women of Montgomery will call for a boycott to take place on Monday, December 5."

–JO ANN ROBINSON

This woman's case will come up on Monday. We are, therefore, asking every Negro to stay off the buses Monday in protest of the arrest and trial. Don't ride the buses to work, to town, to school, or anywhere on Monday. You can afford to stay out of school for one day if you have no other way to go except by bus. You can also afford to stay out of town for one day. If you work, take a cab, or walk. But please, children and grown-ups, don't ride the bus at all on Monday. Please stay off all buses Monday."

Robinson and the two students spent the remainder of the hours before they had to be in class at 8 a.m. mapping out distribution routes for the messages. After class, Robinson called other

At that meeting, attended by about 50 people, the decision was made that a mass meeting to which all blacks in the city would be invited would be held Monday night, December 5, at Holt Street Baptist Church, where the Rev. A.W. Wilson was pastor. The Rev. W.J. Powell agreed to organize cabs and private cars to offer rides to blacks on Monday. King led a committee which

The Rev. Ralph Abernathy, who was instrumental in organizing the bus boycott, expresses his outrage over the policy of segregated public buses.
Don Cravens/Time Life Pictures/Getty Images

OFFICE OF
THE MONTGOMERY IMPROVEMENT ASSOCIATION
725 DORSEY STREET
PHONE 5-3364 OR 3-9153
MASS MEETING
MOUNT ZION A.M.E. ZION CHURCH
MONDAY JANUARY 16, 1956
7:00 P.M.
****
Presiding Officer ---- pastor of Mt.Zion A.M.E. Rev. L. R. Bennett
Opening Hymn -------------------------- "Onward Christian Soldier"
Scripture ------------------------- 1st Corinthians; 13th Chapter
                          Rev. S.S. Seay, Mt. Zion and Rogers Chapel (Elmo
Prayer -------------------------- Dr. H.H. Hubbard, Pastor Beth
                                   Baptist Church
Hymn ------------------------------ "Yield Not To Temptation"
Opening Remarks -------------------- Rev. L. R. Bennett
Transportation Committee Report ----- Mr. R. A. Lewis
Pep Talk --------------------------- Dr. Reva W. Allman
Appeal ----------------------------- Mrs. Fannie A. Neal
Offering --------------------------- Rev. A. W. Bonner
                                      Pastor First C.M.E. Chur
Announcements ----------------------
Closing Hymn ---------------------- "Blest Be The Tie"
Benediction ----------------------- Rev. U. J. Fields

Thursday Nite Mass Meetings
January 19, 1956 at 7:00 P. M.
At the Following Churches
Please Be Present

The First Baptist Church, Greater Washington Park
Pastor, R. Joe T. Thomas

King Hill Baptist Church, King Hill
Pastor, Rev. W. M. McCloud

North Montgomery Baptist Church, 1519 Ferguson Street
Pastor, Rev. A.W. Murphy

Peoples Baptist Church, 1522 Carrie Street
Pastor, Rev. J. J. Rose

ARE YOU A VOTER?

"Just Think, What it Means If You Were"

MASS MEETING
Montgomery Improvement Association
Dr. M. L. King, Jr., President
Holt Street Baptist Church
Rev. A. W. Wilson, Pastor
Monday, September 24, 1956 - 7p.m.
Mr. Nathaniel Smith, Presiding
Mrs. Odallian Garnier, General Chairman
********* YAD'S SPONSORS *********

1. Opening Song ... "Leaning On the Everlasting Arm" ...... Audience
2. Prayer .... Rev. Robert Graetz
3. Occasion .... Mrs. Inez J. Baskin
4. Remarks .... Rev. M. L. King., Jr.
5. Offering .... Finance Committee of M. I. A.
                                                   Rev. R. J. Glasco, Chairman
6. Transportation Observations .... Rev. B. J. Simms, Chairman
                                            Transportation Committee
7. Voting Committee .... Mr. F. L. Massey
8. Program Observations .... Rev. Ralph D. Abernathy
   Announcements
9. Song .... Senior Choir of Holt Street
                                                   Baptist Church
10. Pep Talk .... Atty. Fred D. Gray
11. Solo .... Mr. J. C. Murphy
12. Closing Hymn ...... "Bless Be The Tie" .... Audience
13. Benediction .... Rev. J. L. Duvall

Agendas for mass meetings held on January 16, 1956, at Mount Zion AME Zion Church, soon after the bus boycott began, and September 24, 1956, at Holt Street Baptist Church, towards the end. *Alabama State Archives*

added language about the mass meeting to the WPC flier and distributed another 7,000 copies that Saturday.

Recruitment continued over the weekend, with one white minister, the Rev. Robert Graetz, agreeing to help. Graetz pastored the all-black Trinity Lutheran Church. Like black ministers throughout the city, Graetz used his pulpit that Sunday to urge participation in the Monday boycott, as well as to suggest that parishioners with automobiles help provide rides to those who would need them.

Monday, December 5, was filled with milestones: the boycott, the court date for Rosa

A group of women participate in the Montgomery Bus Boycott. *Don Cravens/TimeLife Pictures/Getty Images*

Parks, the initial meeting of what would become the Montgomery Improvement Association, and a mass meeting where history was made.

The weather cooperated that Monday morning, dawning cold but clear. Normally the morning buses would be crowded with blacks heading to work throughout the city, but only a handful of blacks were waiting at bus stops, most of them elderly.

Instead, many blacks gathered near the stops, waiting for rides. Interestingly, many of those rides came from whites whose primary interest was getting their employees, including many domestic workers, to their homes or places of business. Other blacks rode Negro taxis, with many drivers giving reduced fares that day. Thousands more walked to work and school. Participation far exceeded the best hopes of the boycott leaders. Many white riders also avoided the buses that day, although it is likely the vast majority feared trouble rather than sympathizing with the boycott.

The Rev. Martin Luther King Jr.'s passionate speeches at the mass meetings stirred the emotions of the black community and united them in a common cause—integrated public buses in Montgomery.
Montgomery Advertiser files

Merchants in the 1950s were concentrated downtown, and the bus boycott had a major impact on business there, since buses were the primary means of transportation for blacks and for many whites. Montgomery's white leadership could not help but notice that despite the Christmas buying season being in full swing, almost no blacks and many fewer whites than normal shopped downtown that Monday.

Robinson later related in her memoir the story of a black woman who had walked "halfway across town" before being given a ride by a minister, who asked if she was tired. She replied, "Well, my body may be a bit tired, but for many years now my soul has been tired. Now my soul is resting. So I don't mind if my body is tired, because my soul is free."

Meanwhile that Monday, Rosa Parks was appearing in court.

Like Claudette Colvin before her, Parks had not technically violated the bus ordinance. During her trial, that point was never mentioned by the city prosecutor, D. Eugene Loe. Loe said later of the case: "It was a routine case that just came up. We didn't pay any attention to it. It wasn't a cause celebre one way or another in court."

But Parks's attorney, Fred Gray, saw the 30-minute trial differently. He knew that because Parks was charged with disorderly conduct, the trial was not the best venue to mount a challenge against bus segregation. However, the trial, his first before a large audience, still had a huge personal significance for him. That was partly because his client also was his friend, but also because he suspected that it was the opening salvo in a case that would allow him an opportunity "to raise legal issues that ultimately would be decided by the United States Supreme Court."

The Rev. Martin Luther King Jr., president of the Montgomery Improvement Association, outlines bus boycott strategies to his advisers and fellow organizers, including the Rev. Ralph Abernathy (seated, left) and Rosa Parks (seated, middle).
Don Cravens/Time Life Pictures/Getty Images

Despite the constitutional issues raised by Gray, Judge John B. Scott found Parks guilty and fined her $10 plus $4 in court costs, thus giving another nudge to the mounting desire in the black community for action.

In midafternoon, 16 to 18 people gathered in the pastor's study of the Mt. Zion AME Zion Church to discuss strategies. The ad hoc leaders of the movement seemed to agree that a new organization was needed to lead the boycott effort if it was to continue. While most of the leaders already were members of the NAACP, it was felt that a new organization was needed, for several reasons. One was that the NAACP was reviled by many whites and already under attack in state courts, and it was feared that it would serve as a lightning rod to arouse opposition to the protest. And a new group would keep the leadership effort at the local level.

The Rev. Ralph Abernathy suggested the name "Montgomery Improvement Association," and it was adopted.

African-American laborers walk to work during the third month of a bus boycott that lasted 381 days.
Don Cravens/Time Life Pictures/Getty Images

> "But I want to tell you this evening that it is not enough for us to talk about love. Love is one of the pivotal points of the Christian faith. There is another side called justice. And justice is really love in calculation. Justice is love correcting that which revolts against love."
>
> —MARTIN LUTHER KING JR.

Care was also taken in the selection of the MIA's leadership. Discussions of who would be the best spokesman for the boycott effort had been part of the give and take throughout the weekend. Gray and Robinson recalled in their books on the boycott that they had discussed Robinson's minister, Martin Luther King Jr., with E.D. Nixon. Knowing that there already existed cliques in the black community and resentments over roles, there was a consensus that a new face was necessary to lead the MIA. That person turned out to be King.

In addition, a resolutions committee was formed, chaired by Abernathy and with Fred Gray as a member.

Gray reported that blacks started gathering as early as 3 p.m. for the mass meeting at Holt Street Baptist Church scheduled for 7 p.m., where King was set to give the opening address, his first as a civil rights leader.

Gray later wrote that he had prepared two resolutions for that evening: one in case that day's boycott had failed, which called for negotiations with city officials to resolve differences, and another in case the boycott was a success, calling for all black citizens of Montgomery to not ride the buses until they were desegregated. The first resolution clearly was not needed.

King's speech stirred the thousand or more people packed into every cranny of the church. He urged them to use Christian love as a tool to protect their rights: "But I want to tell you this evening that it is not enough for us to talk about love. Love is one of the pivotal points of the Christian faith. There is another side called justice. And justice is really love in calculation. Justice is love correcting that which revolts against love."

Buoyed by the success of that day's boycott and by King's rousing speech, the audience rose and cheered in support of the resolution to continue the boycott.

The historic Montgomery Bus Boycott had begun.

The First Mass Meeting

The late *Montgomery Advertiser* city editor Joe Azbell, who had a longstanding working relationship with black civil rights activist E.D. Nixon, broke the story on the front page of the newspaper's Sunday, December 4, edition about a planned one-day boycott on Monday, which helped to spread the word of the boycott throughout the black community. Azbell also wrote the news story and a column on the first mass meeting, held on Monday evening, at which blacks voted to continue the boycott.

In the news story, Azbell wrote: "An estimated 5,000 hymn-singing Negroes packed the Holt Street Baptist Church to its outer doors and spilled over into three streets blocking traffic last night as they voted to continue a racial boycott against buses of the Montgomery City Lines Inc."

He described those attending the mass meeting as adopting a resolution "with a roaring applause," asking that all citizens of Montgomery "refrain from riding buses of the Montgomery City Lines Inc. until the bus transportation situation is cleared up to the 'satisfaction of citizens' who ride and patronize them."

The city editor quoted the Rev. Martin Luther King Jr., pastor of the Dexter Avenue Baptist Church, as urging the black community to "stick together and work together if we are to win, and we will win in standing up for our rights as Americans." Of the boycott itself, Azbell wrote in the news story: "Negroes stood on downtown street corners waiting for rides or piled into taxicabs. Many walked two or three miles to work in the crisp, cold weather. Most Negro children walked to school, and there was a relay auto pickup system operating through-out most of the day."

Here is Azbell's column describing the first mass meeting:

AT HOLT STREET BAPTIST CHURCH: DEEPLY STIRRED THRONG OF COLORED CITIZENS PROTEST BUS SEGREGATION

By Joe Azbell

As I drove along Cleveland Avenue en route to the Holt Street Baptist Church Monday night, I could see Negroes by the dozens forming a file,

The Weather

Montgomery: Cloudy to partly cloudy and continued cool. Predicted high today 54, low 38. High yesterday 57, low 43. (Details, Weather Map, Page 3A.)

The Montgomery Adv

127th Year—No. 291

Full Day, Night and Sunday Service
By The Associated Press

Montgomery, Ala., Tuesday Morning, December 6, 1955

5,000 At Meeting Outline Boycott; Bullet Clips Bus

By JOE AZBELL
Advertiser City Editor

An estimated 5,000 hymn-singing Negroes packed the Holt Street Baptist Church to its outer doors and spilled over into three streets blocking traffic last night as they voted to continue a racial boycott against buses of the Montgomery City Lines Inc.

Meanwhile, J. H. Bagley, manager of the Montgomery City Lines, reported that a bus driven by driver B. S. Johnson, apparently was fired on by a person with a 22 caliber rifle in the Negro Washington Park area.

Bagley said the bullet hit the rear of the bus and Johnson could not determine from where it was fired.

Regents Give Georgia Tech 'Green Light'

ATLANTA, Dec. 5.—Georgia's Board of Regents today rejected Gov. Marvin Griffin's move to have Georgia Tech's football team pulled from the Sugar Bowl on a racial issue and opened the way for non-segregated games played outside the South.

At the same time, it closed the door on any further bowl games played in the South, which do not follow the segregation laws and customs of the host state.

This was a direct slap at the Sugar Bowl officials who not only invited Pittsburgh, a team with a Negro player, to meet Tech, but also let Pittsburgh sell its tickets on a nonsegregated basis.

BACKED DOWN

Shortly before the regents acted, Griffin had backed down somewhat on his Friday demand for a racial policy that not only would have barred Tech from the Sugar Bowl but would have prohibited any Georgia state college teams from playing against Negroes or before unsegregated spectators.

The governor told his news conference that his request to the regents chairman, Robert O. Arnold of Covington, was aimed only at the Sugar Bowl and that he would

ENFORCE LAW

The bus company manager also reiterated a previous statement that his firm would not violate the law on segregation of bus passengers and that he would continue to require all of his drivers to enforce the law. "If they don't, the drivers can be fined or sentenced," he said.

Meanwhile, police reported an unidentified party threw a large stone and struck the front of a City Lines bus at the intersection of S. Jeff Davis and S. Holt street late yesterday. No personal injury and only slight damage to the bus resulted, officers said.

In a resolution passed at the meeting by the Negroes with a roaring applause, the emotional group voted to ask "all citizens of Montgomery" to refrain from riding buses of the Montgomery City Lines Inc. until the bus transportation situation is cleared up to the "satisfaction of citizens" who ride and patronize them.

The resolution, among other things, stated that "citizens of Montgomery" have been intimidated, embarrassed and coerced while riding the public conveyances and in view of the humiliation they have endured they agreed that they would refrain from using the buses.

It also declared that a "delegation of citizens" was prepared at all times to sit down with officials of the Montgomery City Lines and

NEGROES TO CONTINUE BOYCOTT

An estimated crowd of 5,000 Negroes roared approval to a resolution last night at the Holt Street Baptist Church to continue a boycott against the Montgomery City Lines, Inc. until the bus situation is settled to the satisfaction of its patrons. The huge assemblage featured the appearance of Rosa Parks, 42-year-old Negro woman, who was convicted yesterday of violating segregation laws by refusing to move from the white section of a city bus to the Negro section under orders of the bus driver.—*Photo by Lesher.*

LONE NEGRO WAITS AT BUS STOP

Vot Kin Ove

Education Top Two To Face

By BOB IN

Alabama voters decision today on amendments to the tion, including two signed to solve problems of education.

Tremendous interest aroused in the re most of it centered ments No. 1 and 2 school tax and the bond issue.

But also up for co four other amendments wide application a ments applying to ties and cities.

ADJUSTED INCOM

The school tax p after its author, Re Goodwyn of Montg — would levy a tax gross income of corporations.

Goodwyn and o State Revenue De estimated the tax produce approxima lion annually, all o exclusively for edu

Supporters of the the Citizens Schools, have warn nue sought by this provided the schoo will close in March

This charge has denied by opponen and Gov. James one occasion state

The front page of the December 6, 1955, edition of the *Montgomery Advertiser* features an article and photos covering the first boycott meeting.
Montgomery Advertiser files

Boycott leaders the Rev. H.H. Johnson (second from left), E.D. Nixon (second from right), and the Rev. A.W. Wilson (right) wait their turn to speak after the Rev. Martin Luther King Jr. (left).
Montgomery Advertiser files

almost soldierly, on the sidewalk. They were going to the Rosa Parks protest meeting at the church.

They were silent people, bundled in overcoats, performing what appeared to be a ritual. I parked my automobile a block from the church and noted the time was 6:45. Already cars were strung out for six or seven blocks in each direction.

In fact, the area around the church looked like Cramton Bowl at an Alabama State-Tuskegee football game. Except for one thing: These people were stony silent.

The Negroes eyed me and one inquired if I was a policeman. He turned to his three companions: "He says he ain't the law." I walked up to the steps of the church and two Negro policemen were standing there chatting. Both were courteous when I introduced myself, and one went inside and found out about the seating arrangement for the press. Chairs were placed down front for the reporters. The TV cameraman from WSFA-TV and the United Press reporter later took these seats. I stood in the rear of the church during the meeting while reporter Steve Lesher anchored himself in a chair near the church's pulpit.

The inside of the church is impressive because of its simplicity. The church has the ordinary equipment of the upper-middle class white church, and there's a large mirror across the back wall.

I observed police squad cars parked two blocks away in each direction from the church, and occasionally a police sergeant would drive by and check with the four Negro policemen who were handling the traffic at the church.

FURTHER INSTRUCTIONS

I went inside the church and stood at the front for a few minutes. The two rear doors were jammed with people, and a long aisle was crammed with human forms like a frozen food package. I went to the rear of the church and it was the same. The Negro policemen pleaded with the

Negroes to keep the aisles free so people could get out. In the end the policemen gave up in despair of correcting the safety hazard. Bodies at the front were packed one against the other. It required five minutes for a photographer to move eight feet among these people in trying to leave the building.

The purpose of this meeting was to give further instructions on the boycott of city buses, which had been started as a protest of the Negroes against the arrest, trial, and conviction of Rosa Parks, 42-year-old seamstress, on a charge of violating segregation laws by refusing to give up her seat to a white person and move to the rear of a city bus.

There were four white reporters or photographers at the meeting. Only one other white person attended. He appeared to be a young college student or airman, and he came with a Negro and left with a Negro. He sat in the group of Negroes in the balcony.

The Rev. Solomon Seay addresses bus boycotters at a mass meeting. *Montgomery Advertiser files*

Greg Villet/Time Life Pictures/Getty Images

Members of the black community fill Holl Street Baptist Church during the bus boycott.
Montgomery Advertiser files

SPEAKERS UNIDENTIFIED

The meeting was started in a most unusual fashion. A Negro speaker—apparently a minister—came to the microphone. He did not introduce himself but apparently most of the Negroes knew him. He said there were microphones on the outside and in the basement, and there were three times as many people outside as on the inside. There was an anonymity throughout the meeting of the speakers. None of the white reporters could identify the speakers. Most of the Negroes did. The introductions of Fred Daniels and Rosa Parks were clear and brief. Daniels was arrested in the boycott Monday.

WHITES LISTEN

The passion that fired the meeting was seen as the thousands of voices joined in singing "Onward, Christian Soldiers." Another hymn followed. The voices thundered through the church.

Then there followed a prayer by a minister. It was a prayer interrupted a hundred times by "yeas" and "uh-huhs" and "that's right." The minister spoke of God as the Master and the brotherhood of man. He repeated in a different way that God would protect the righteous.

As the other speakers came on the platform urging "freedom and equality" for Negroes "who are Americans and proud of this democracy," the frenzy of the audience mounted. There was a volume of clapping that seemed to boom through the walls. Outside the loudspeakers were blaring the message for blocks. White people stopped blocks away and listened to the loudspeakers' messages.

THE HAT IS PASSED

The newspapers were criticized for quoting police authorities on reports of intimidation of Negroes who attempted to ride buses and for comparing the Negro boycott with the economic reprisals of White Citizens groups.

The remark which drew the most applause was: "We will not retreat one inch in our fight to secure and hold our American citizenship." Second was a statement: "And the history book will write of us as a race of people who in Montgomery County, State of Alabama, Country of the United States, stood up for and fought for their rights as American citizens, as citizens of democracy." Outside the audience listened as more and more cars continued to arrive. Streets became...traffic snarls. There was hymn singing between speeches. In the end there was the passing of the hats, and

Negroes dropped in dollar bills, $5 bills and $10 bills. It was not passive giving but active giving. Negroes called to the hat passers outside, "Here, let me give."

PEACEFUL MEANS

When the resolution on continuing the boycott of the bus was read, there came a wild whoop of delight. Many said they would never ride the bus again. Negroes turned to each other and compared past incidents on the buses.

(continued on page 48)

Boycott supporters clap in time with the music—a major part of each mass meeting. *Montgomery Advertiser files*

The Rev. Martin Luther King Jr. addresses those gathered for the mass meeting at Holt Street Baptist Church. *Montgomery Advertiser files*

Montgomery's black community participates in a mass meeting at Holt Street Baptist Church.
Montgomery Advertiser files

A supporter of the bus boycott prays during a mass meeting. *Grey Villet/Time Life Pictures/Getty Images*

At several points there was emotionalism that the ministers on the platform recognized could get out of control and at various intervals they repeated again and again what "we are seeking is by peaceful means."

"There will be no violence or intimidation. We are seeking things in a democratic way, and we are using the weapon of protest," the speakers declared.

MORE HYMNS

I left as the meeting was breaking up. The Negroes made a path for me through the crowd as I went to my car, but the packed group found it uncomfortable to move. A cry of fire would have caused a panic that could have resulted in scores of deaths. Negroes on the outside recognized this danger, but these people wanted to see and hear what was going on.

There was hymn singing as I drove away. At the first corner where I turned, I nodded at the policemen in a squad car. At the next corner I saw another squad car. And at the next corner where I stopped for a signal light, the driver of another squad car asked if the meeting had ended.

The meeting was much like an old-fashioned revival with loud applause added. It proved beyond any doubt there was a discipline among Negroes that many whites had doubted. It was almost a military discipline combined with emotion.

The mass meetings, held at local churches during the bus boycott, were often emotional as leaders called upon the community to unite against segregation. *Montgomery Advertiser files*

A woman speaks from the audience during a bus boycott meeting.
Montgomery Advertiser files

Violence
and Intimidation

The Montgomery Bus Boycott that began on December 5, 1955, would last for 381 days, a span during which life for virtually every black Montgomerian changed dramatically.

It may be difficult 50 years or more after the boycott for younger Americans to grasp just how a bus boycott could so fundamentally affect the lives of so many residents of a city. The bus system was the primary means of transportation for the majority of black citizens, who owned relatively few private vehicles. Researchers estimate that some 17,000 blacks took part in the boycott initially, although the numbers quickly grew because of action by the bus system itself. Shortly after the boycott ended, the Rev. Martin Luther King Jr. claimed that 42,000 blacks took part.

A few days after the boycott began, bus officials asked the City Commission for permission to close routes to many of the primary black communities, arguing that the boycott had made service to those areas no longer financially attractive. So in those parts of town, even the handful of blacks who might have wanted to use the buses could not do so.

Several black taxi companies existed in the city, and for the first few days of the boycott these helped to absorb former bus riders looking for alternative transportation. Boycott leaders persuaded most of these companies to charge only 10 cents per ride during the hours most blacks were going to and coming from work. But a few days into the boycott, city officials started to enforce a previously ignored city ordinance that set minimum fares at 45 cents. That priced taxi rides on a daily basis out of the reach of many blue-collar blacks.

Motorcycle police keep tabs on a small crowd of blacks who are waiting for a car pool lift during the bus boycott.
Don Cravens/Time Life Pictures/Getty Images

Georgette Norman, now the director of the Rosa Parks Museum at Troy University in Montgomery, was nine years old during the boycott. While she did not have to routinely walk to school because her family had a car, she does recall a day that "everybody was supposed to walk, whether you had a car or not."

"We lived on the west side, but I went to school on the east side. My father and mother worked on the east side, so it meant that we had to walk from the west side to the east side. I recall that it was really fun because you would meet people along the way."

The boycott wasn't fun for most adult African Americans in Montgomery. Not only were many concerned about losing their jobs because they could not get to work, but also they feared that some employers would retaliate simply because they took part in the boycott.

Norman remembers that her own father, who managed Tulane Court, a city housing project, received such a threat of retaliation after he attended a mass meeting.

"They called my father and told him that they understood he attended a mass meeting the night before, and that if he valued his job he would not be going to any more meetings," she said.

At the urging of black churches, blacks who owned cars gave rides to friends and neighbors. Johnnie Carr, a friend of Rosa Parks who served as president of the post-boycott Montgomery Improvement Association for more than three decades, recalls spending time each day giving people rides.

Montgomery's black citizens brave the elements while walking to work.
Greg Villet/Time Life Pictures/Getty Images

A police officer issues a parking ticket during the bus boycott.
Don Cravens/Time Life Pictures/Getty Images

"We had people who would walk miles to get to their destination rather than ride the buses," Carr said. "My husband and I both had cars since we were in the insurance business, and we would go by on the way to work to see if we could drop anybody off." Hundreds of other middle-class blacks—pastors, doctors, teachers and college professors—did the same.

Interestingly, early in the boycott many white citizens also helped provide transportation to and from work for their black employees, especially domestic workers. While a few whites supported the boycott, most of them were motivated either by sympathy to the plight of their black employees or just wanted their work to be done.

But over time, the number of whites providing transportation dwindled under pressure from others in the white community. The varied social and business pressures brought against sympathetic whites were captured by the 1990 movie, *The Long Walk Home*, starring Whoopi Goldberg and Sissy Spacek.

Boycott leaders quickly realized that their plans for a more organized alternative transportation system would have to be put into high gear if the boycott were to succeed long term.

Churches bought cars and station wagons specifically for the transportation system. Pick-up and delivery points were designated around the city and routes were established. People who needed gasoline were provided fuel. The city police harassed the system by enforcing laws against crowding and a variety of minor traffic violations, but the car pool succeeded anyway. It soon developed into an efficient and cost-effective means of transportation, with some observers noting ironically that it solved several of the transportation problems with which the bus system had struggled for years.

As the boycott wore on, intimidation tactics took various forms. The most sweeping official action designed to deter boycott leaders came in February 1956, when the Montgomery grand jury indicted 89 boycott leaders—including King, Parks, Abernathy and most of the other participating black ministers. The charges were based on a 1921 state statute that barred boycotts without "just cause." Those indicted were arrested over the next few days, booked and released on bond.

(continued on page 58)

"We had people who would walk miles to get to their destination rather than ride the buses."

—JOHNNIE CARR

Above: Boycott supporters exit a Bell Street Baptist Church station wagon on June 12, 1956. The car was one of dozens used in the car pool that served as transportation during the bus boycott. *Montgomery Advertiser files*

Previous page: Blacks car pool during the bus boycott. Note the empty bus in the background. *Don Cravens/Time Life Pictures/Getty Images*

But as official tactics failed to discourage the boycott, unofficial intimidation soon took a more dangerous turn. In January, the parsonage in which King and his family lived was bombed. Coretta Scott King and the Kings' two-year-old daughter Yolanda narrowly escaped injury. King stood on his damaged porch and persuaded an angry crowd of blacks, some of them armed, not to respond with violence. The next night, E.D. Nixon's home was also bombed.

In August, the home of white Lutheran minister Robert Graetz also was bombed. Graetz, whose church was all-black, was probably targeted because he was the only white member of the board of the Montgomery Improvement Association. His home was later bombed again.

Graetz said his greatest concern was for his children, especially after he and his wife received anonymous calls pointedly mentioning what his children had been doing just moments before. The callers were trying to intimidate Graetz by showing that his children were under observation and vulnerable.

Graetz's wife, Jeannie, said: "I had the feeling they were just out to scare us and nothing bad would happen. I had to make myself feel that way."

(continued on page 63)

These booking photos were taken in February 1956 during the mass arrest of 89 boycott leaders for violating the state anti-boycott law—(clockwlse from top left) the Rev. Martin Luther King Jr., the Rev. Ralph D. Abernathy and attorney Fred Gray. *Montgomery County Archives*

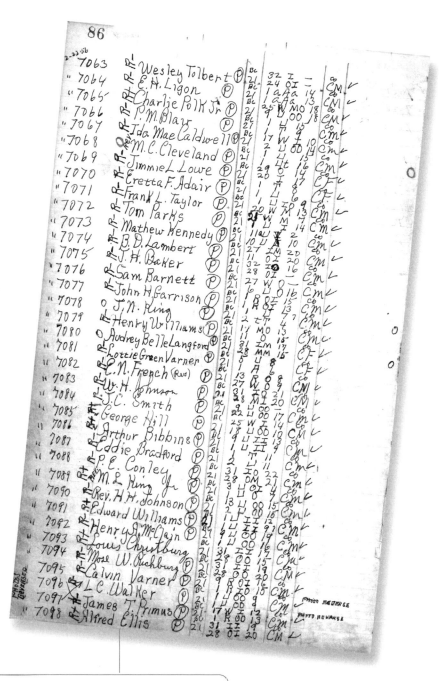

These pages from the booking log show many of the names of the 89 boycott leaders arrested in February 1956: the Rev. M.L. King Jr., Rosa Parks, E.D. Nixon, Jo Ann Robinson, and Fred D. Gray, among others. *Montgomery County Archives*

"Dr. King used to talk about the reality that some of us were going to die, and that if any of us were afraid to die we really shouldn't be there."

–ROBERT S. GRAETZ

The Rev. Graetz said that in the end, they simply had to trust in God to protect them.

Even past the end of the boycott, the violence continued. In addition to bombings, King's home was shot into. After the boycott came to a close, snipers shot into buses in black communities, at one point hitting a young black woman, Rosa Jordan, in the legs. Her injuries were not life-threatening.

Standing before the state Capitol are the 89 indicted boycott leaders, just after arraignment and pleading not guilty to conspiracy charges.
Don Cravens/Time Life Pictures/Getty Images

The worst single night of violence occurred on January 10, 1957, a few weeks after the end of the boycott and segregated seating on buses. Four black churches and two homes were bombed, including the Rev. Ralph Abernathy's church and parsonage.

"Dr. King used to talk about the reality that some of us were going to die, and that if any of us were afraid to die we really shouldn't be there," Graetz said.

But amazingly, King was wrong. Despite the violence, no one died in the boycott, and only Rosa Jordan was shot.

The intimidation tactics failed to significantly deter any black boycotters. Instead, for the most part, they spurred black Montgomerians to greater efforts.

(continued on page 69)

THURSDAY, FEBRUARY 23, 1956

★ THE MONTGOMERY ADVERTI

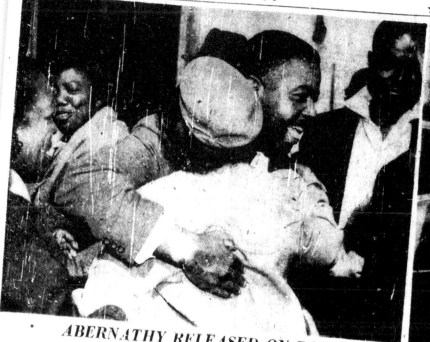

ABERNATHY RELEASED ON BOND

A member of First Baptist Church hugs the Rev. Ralph Abernathy, pastor, after he was released on bond at the county jail yesterday. A large crowd of his "flock" greeted the minister, who is director of the Alabama Negro Baptist Center, as he left the jail.—Photo by AP

FIRST TWO ARRESTED

The first two Negro ministers to be arrested yest county jail after they were booked and fingerprinted deputies. They were Rev. Ralph D. Abernathy (left) a H. Hoffman.—Photo by AP

BOYCOTT LEADERS AT JAIL

Four of the outstanding leaders in the boycott of Montgomery City Lines buses by Negroes pause as they leave county jail after being booked yesterday in connection with the boycott. They are (left to right) Rev. L. R. Bennett, Rev. H. H. Hubbard, Rev. Ralph D. Abernathy and E. D. Nixon. Behind the quartet is Ben Burton, who posted bond for the men —Photo by AP

MINISTER FINGERPRINTED

The Rev. Martin Luther King Jr. enters an automobile soon after his home was bombed.
Montgomery Advertiser files

Rosa Jordan, an African American who was hit in the legs by a bullet fired into a city bus a few days after the boycott ended, filed this report with police.
Courtesy of the Rosa Parks Museum, Troy University

OAK STREET GENERAL HOSPITAL
ADDIE B. PAYNE, R.N., Superintendent

910 Oak St. — Phone 8474
Montgomery 5, Alabama
December 28, 1956

I, Rosa Jordan make the following statement to detectives K.W.Jones and J.C.McKenzie of my own free will without promise of reward or threat of injury to myself

Tonight, Dec. 28,1956 I was riding home on the Boylston bus and was sitting near the rear of the buss. As we neared Ripley street on Cloumbus St I heard a noise that sounded like a shot and a bullet hit me in both legs.

I was sitting with my back to the street and did not see where the shot came from.

The bus driver stopped and called an ambulance and the police and they took me to the Oak Street Hospital for treatment.

I have read the above statement and it is true to the best of my knowledge and I willingly sign my name:

SIGNED _Rosa Jordan_
ROSA JORDAN
1546 WITHERS STREET

WITNESSES _K.W. Jones_
K.W. JONES
J.C. McKenzie
J.C. MCKENZIE

SOLD

PHILCO console combination 21"
radio-record player in beautiful
hogany cabinet. Entire set in per
condition. No antenna needed. Ori
cost, $675, now $275 cash. 3220 Mon
zuma.

DIAL 4-4567
The Fast Magic Number
Want Ads Can Help You, To

...mery, Ala., Tuesday Morning, January 31, 1956 | 44 Pages | Price 5 Cents

Blast Rocks Residence Of Bus Boycott Leader

...nson Faces ...ew Troubles ...ith Congress

...uzzles Suggestion ...or Assistants ...o Eisenhower

By WILMOT HERCHER

...ASHINGTON, Jan. 30 (AP)—Sec-
...y of Agriculture Benson came
...r fresh fire in Congress to-
...with Rep. Burdick (R-SD)
...esting that Benson and some
... Cabinet members should
...r muzzles."

...mands for Benson's resigna-
...arose last week after publica-
...of a letter, signed with his
...e, applauding a magazine ar-
...which called the American
...er "our pampered tyrant."
...nson's apologetic statement
...y that the letter to the editor
...arper's magazine was a staff
...er" added to the uproar on
...ol Hill.

...RAGE SHOWED

...t Sen. Bennett (R-Utah) told
...Senate the secretary's frank
...owledgement of the error
...d courage and should per
...e critics to withdraw their de-
...is that he resign.

...rdick issued a statement sug-
...ng that some members of
...dent Eisenhower's Cabinet
... suffering from "hoof and
...h disease."

...very time they open their
...h" Burdick said, "they seem
...t their foot in it."

... said the President should in-
...that these men wear muzzles,
...ugh he said he doubted wheth-
...muzzles "would stop the ap-
...ance of letters in the maga-
... under the name of a secre-
...who never saw or read or
...d the publication."

...SON'S 'BONER'

...nson's "boner" letter was
...en after Harper's published
...article by John Fischer enti-
..."The country slickers take us
...." Benson's note was in reply
...letter written by Horace A
...yles, the magazine's public re-
...s representative, saying he
...ght Benson might like to see
...rticle "in support of your po-

...the department letter said.
...ave read the article by John
...er in the December issue of
...er's with a great deal of in-
... It is excellent."

... Morse (D-Ore) said he
...ht the article was "a pretty
...rate reflection of Mr. Benson's
...ultural policy," and that he
... propose to accept the sec-
...rticle at its "face va...

SCENE OF BOMBED HOME

These are the shattered front windows of the home of the Rev. M. L. King, Negro boycott
leader, at 309 S. Jackson St. that was bombed last night. It was believed a hand grenade or a
half stick of dynamite was tossed or placed on the front porch. The bomb shattered the front
windows, ripped a mailbox from the wall, and split a pillar on the porch.

KING ADDRESSES NEGRO CROWD

The Rev. M. L. King, Negro boycott leader, addresses the large crowd that formed outside his home at 309 S. Jackson St. last night after the house was bombed. He told the Negroes
"not to get your weapons, be peaceful, and remember if I am stopped, this movement will
not be stopped." Left to right are Fire Chief R. L. Lampley, Mayor W. A. Gayle, King, and

None Injured After Bombin... Of King Hom...

By JOE AZBELL
Advertiser City Editor

A bomb tossed on the porch
the home of the Rev. M. L. K...
Negro boycott leader, 309 S. J...
son St. about 9:15 last night s...
tered windows, ripped a hole...
the porch and cracked a p...
column. No one was injured

Neighbors reported that a...
colored automobile was seen
the time of the explosion. It...
believed to have stopped in f...
of the home as a man got...
and placed or tossed the b...
on the porch.

Coretta King, wife of the...
tist minister, said she was si...
in the front room of the six-r...
white frame dwelling a half b...
from the Ben Moore Hotel w...
she heard footsteps and a...
"like a brick hitting on the por...

She said she was talking...
the wife of Roscoe Williams, M...
gomery electrician, and that...
feared the "thud" might...
"something dangerous." The...
women ducked through a side...
to the middle bedroom and...
to a third room in the rear...
they reached the third room,...
said that they heard the explo...

In the rear room also was...
Kings' seven and a half week...
baby, Yolanda Denise

Vann Pruitt, assistant state...
cologist, said he believed the b...
to be either a hand grenade...
half stick of dynamite.

HOLE IN CONCRETE

The bomb hit on the south...
of the porch about two feet...
the concrete steps. It ripp...
slight hole about a half...
deep, four inches long and...
inches wide in the tile-like p...
covering.

The bomb explosion shat...
the four windows on the fro...
the house, sending glass...
inside the living room on the...
side and den and music roo...
the south side. The house i...
parsonage of Dexter Avenue...
tist Church.

The house is about 15 feet

ntgomery Advertiser

Montgomery, Ala., Saturday Morning, December 29, 1956

Up To The Minute On The Spot! Advertiser-Journal Telephone News Service, Dial 5-8246

16 Pages

Price 5 Cents

Sniper Fires On Bus; Wounds Negro Woman

Officials Halt Transit Line After Attacks

By BOB MURPHY

A Negro woman was shot in both legs here last night by a sniper's bullet which slammed into a city bus from ambush on Columbus Avenue near Bainbridge Street. The bus was carrying 12 white and Negro passengers.

SIX OF EACH RACE

The same bus was fired on a short time later as it resumed its run after inspection and passenger interrogation at police headquarters. No one was injured in the second shooting.

After an emergency meeting of the City Commission, Police Commissioner W. A. Gayle told The Advertiser early this morning that an emergency meeting of the city commission will be held today to decide what to do concerning the bus-shooting incidents. "We don't condone violence. Law and order must be preserved," he said. "That is why we stopped the buses last night." The buses will continue to run today, the mayor said.

missioner Clyde Sellers ordered all bus runs suspended for the remainder of the night. They were expected to resume normal operations today under stricter police supervision.

DRIVER CHECKS BULLET HOLE IN BUS
William H. Fullilove, 2805 Locust St.

PASSENGERS GET ABOARD BOYLSTON BUS
At Police Station Fo'lowing Shooting Incident

Resort Swept | BUS CONTROVERSY SPREADS

U Of A Board

In an analysis of the Montgomery Bus Boycott printed in the journal *Liberation* in 1957, King wrote: "Because the mayor and city authorities cannot admit to themselves that we [black Montgomerians] have changed, every move they have made has inadvertently increased the protest and united the Negro community."

King used his arrest for going 30 mph in a 25 mph zone "just two hours before a mass meeting" as an example, saying that after his arrest "we had to hold seven mass meetings to accommodate the people."

He also said the bombings of his and Nixon's homes "brought moral and financial support from all over the state."

In fact, as the black community stood steadfast against intimidation and violence, support for the cause spread not just over the state, but throughout the nation.

Above: A blast in the early hours of January 10, 1957, heavily damaged Bell Street Baptist Church, one of four churches bombed that morning. *Montgomery Advertiser files*

Previous page: Montgomery law enforcement officers disarm a bomb on January 28, 1957, one of several planted in the wake of the Montgomery Bus Boycott. *Montgomery Advertiser files*

Police Muster Reserves In Wake Of Dynamiting

President Asks Battle Against Inflation Peril

WASHINGTON, Jan. 10 — President Eisenhower summoned the American people today to stand "vigilant guard" against ever-threatening inflation at home and the menace abroad of "armed imperialistic dictatorship."

Reporting to Congress and the country on the State of the Union at this moment in history, Eisenhower urged business and labor leaders to "think well on their responsibility to the American people" and go easy on price and wage boosts that could increase inflationary pressures.

"The national interest," he said, "must take precedence over temporary advantages which may be secured by particular groups at the expense of all the people."

INFLATION PERIL

While the pursuit of human liberty, welfare and progress "has brought us to an unprecedented peak in our economic prosperity," the President said, the danger of inflation "is always present."

On the international scene, he said, the existence of a strongly armed imperialistic dictatorship is a continued threat to the security and peace of the free world and "thus to our own." America, he said, cannot stand "alone and isolated."

Dressed in a conservative gray business suit, Eisenhower stood for 33 minutes before a combined, undemonstrative Senate - House session in the klieg - lit House chamber.

With television and radio transmitting his words over national networks, he took a sort of mellow, moderate, unspectacular approach to problems and issues of the day. For solutions, he pretty much stood pat on things he has recommended in the past.

There were brief warmed-over

(See PRESIDENT, Page 2A)

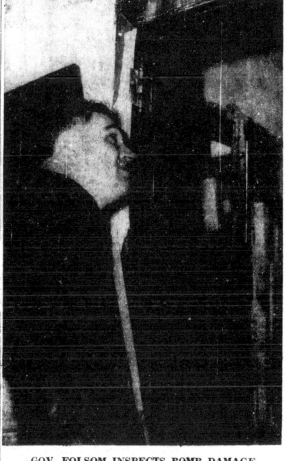

GOV. FOLSOM INSPECTS BOMB DAMAGE
In Dawn Tour of Shattered Churches and Homes

Folsom Posts $2,000 Reward For Information On Bombings

An aroused Gov. James E. Folsom, disturbed by the sudden outbreak of racial violence in Alabama, posted a $2,000 reward yesterday for information leading to the arrest and conviction of the "hoodlums" who dynamited four churches and two homes here early yesterday.

The announcement of the reward was made by Col. Bill Lyerly, director of the Department of Public Safety. Lyerly said the reward also applied in Mobile, where two bombings were reported yesterday.

Noting that the governor deplored the acts of violence, Lyerly quoted Folsom as saying the bombings could have been done by "Negro hoodlums, Communist hoodlums, or by white hoodlums, but whoever did these bombings must certainly be hoodlums."

Gov. Folsom made a personal inspection of the bomb damage inflicted here, being taken on a

Tear Gas, Arms Issued Special Patrol Squads

Every available police reservist has been called to active duty following the pre-dawn bombings of four Negro churches and two homes yesterday, Police Chief G. J. Ruppenthal said last night.

Key officers also shuttled in and out of the chief's office for secret conferences but followed stern instructions not to discuss the case.

Asst. Police Chief Marvin Stanley said reservists and special squads have been issued shotguns, tear gas and rope in a preparedness move.

TOXICOLOGIST'S REPORT

And in another development, Asst. State Toxicologist Vann Pruitt, who has been investigating bomb fragments and other clues, said he will hand his report to Ruppenthal early today.

Meanwhile, all city bus service came to a standstill and Mayor W. A. Gayle may be considering a ban on all inter-racial gatherings such as sporting events. Amateur fights slated for tonight have been cancelled.

At an emergency meeting only a few hours after thousands of Montgomerians had been awakened by the series of jarring explosions, the City Commission ordered a halt to bus operations for an "indefinite" period.

In a separate move indicative of the tense situation, the commission urged a midnight curfew for all teen-agers in Montgomery.

The six blasts that rocked Montgomery caused extensive property damage but no one was injured.

The first blast was reported at approximately 2 a.m. Four other blasts followed in rapid succession in scattered sections of the city. The sixth and final explosion occurred at approximately 4:30 a.m.

MINISTERS' HOMES

The homes bombed were those of two ministers active in the pro-integration movement in the city —the Rev. Robert Graetz, 1104 Cleveland Ave., and the Rev. Ralph Abernathy, 1327 S. Hall St.

The churches damaged in the wave of bombings were the Bell Street Baptist Church, Hutchinson Street Baptist Church, Mt. Olive Baptist Church and the First Baptist Church (Negro).

The first explosion was reported at the home of Abernathy. He was in Atlanta attending a meeting of Negro leaders, but his wife and two-year-old child were both in the home at the time.

Curfew Urged For City Youth By Commission

The City Commission urged a midnight curfew for teen-agers of both races and ordered all bus service halted for an indefinite period following outbursts of violence here yesterday.

Mayor W. A. Gayle and Commissioners Frank Parks and Clyde Sellers took the action at an extraordinary commission meeting yesterday morning spurred by dynamite blasts that rocked four Negro churches and the homes of two leaders of the Negro Montgomery Improvement Assn.

The mayor said the proposed curfew of Montgomery youth was only a safety precaution. He said he did not think that teen-agers were responsible for the bombings.

Earlier yesterday, a City Lines bus had been fired upon with a shotgun. The shooting took place scant hours after the commission had lifted a 5 p.m. curfew placed on city buses as a result of previous shootings.

BOMBINGS DEPLORED

The commission said they deplored the bombings and urged Montgomerians to remain calm while police restored law and order.

"Parents of all teen-age children, white and colored, male and female," were urged by the commission to "know the whereabouts of their children at all times and have them at home by 12 o'clock midnight unless accompanied by a parent.

Bus service is halted, the commission said, to protect "life, limb and property" of city residents.

"This has become necessary because of the firing on a bus last evening, making a total of six such incidents. The suspension is

---

...oy' Skirt Exciting New Style Feature

☆   ☆   ☆   ☆   ☆   ☆   ☆

...ED IN DAYTIME WEAR, COCKTAIL HEM LOWER

SPENCER
...on Editor
...10—When all ...ners use cer...antly in their

1920s and 30s. This morning Hattie Carnegie's collection was notable for her return to the longer length (eight inches from the floor) for the cocktail dresses, her

skirt popular for evening wear, but daytime lengths are still the same.

All the clothes this season seem to emphasize the lady-like look

A PROFILE:
Martin Luther King Jr.

I t has been said that the Montgomery Bus Boycott's most significant contribution to the struggle for civil rights was providing the opportunity for the Rev. Martin Luther King Jr. to rise to national prominence.

That dramatically undervalues the boycott, which did much more than provide a platform for King: It also served as a model for direct local action, helped to further the cause of nonviolence in social confrontation, helped to focus national and world attention on the equal rights struggle, generated a significant legal precedent in the cause of integration, and perhaps most important, provided a tangible victory for the civil rights cause at a time when one was needed.

After the Montgomery Bus Boycott ended, some of those involved in the boycott came to resent, if not King himself, then the focus on King by the national news media. Perhaps the most outspoken of the critics of this focus on King was E.D. Nixon, who had labored in the civil rights struggle in Montgomery for decades before King moved to the community. Nixon often commented later in life that "the boycott made King" and that the people of Montgomery did more for King than King did for them. (These sentiments were echoed in a larger context later by civil rights leader Ella Baker, who worked with King at the Southern Christian Leadership Conference and commented that "the movement made Martin," not the other way around.)

That being said, the Montgomery Bus Boycott was the springboard for King to become the pre-eminent voice of the national civil rights movement for the next dozen years.

Martin Luther King Jr. was born in Atlanta on January 15, 1929. His family roots were deep in both the church and in the equal rights movement. King's grandfather, the Rev. A.D. Williams, was pastor of Ebenezer Baptist Church in Atlanta and was a founder of the city's NAACP chapter. His father, Martin Luther King Sr., also became pastor of Ebenezer. His mother was Alberta Williams King.

After graduating from Morehouse College in Atlanta in 1948, King studied at Crozer Theological Seminary in Pennsylvania, where he was elected president of a predominantly white senior class. He then pursued his Ph.D. at Boston University, completing his course work in 1953 and receiving his doctorate in systematic theology in 1955. It was during his graduate studies that he came to appreciate the nonviolent strategy for social change being promoted by India's Mohandas Gandhi.

(continued on page 78)

The Montgomery Improvement Association chose the Rev. Martin Luther King Jr. to spearhead the bus boycott. *Montgomery Advertiser files*

Martin Luther King Jr., with his advisers, waves to
passing cars.
Don Cravens/Time Life Pictures/Getty Images

The Rev. Martin Luther King Jr. stands in front of
the Dexter Avenue Baptist Church in Montgomery.
New York Times Co./Getty Images

Martin Luther King Jr. and his wife, Coretta Scott King, emerge from the Montgomery courthouse on March 23, 1956, following his trial on charges of conspiring to boycott segregated city buses. King was found guilty and sentenced to 386 days of hard labor and fined $1,000. King immediately appealed.
AFP/Getty Images

In Boston, King met Coretta Scott, and they were married in 1953. The following year King was offered and accepted the pastorate at Dexter Avenue Baptist Church in Montgomery. The church, located on Montgomery's "main street" only a stone's throw from the state Capitol, had a congregation composed of many of the city's black intellectual and social elite, including many school teachers as well as professors at Alabama State Teachers College (now Alabama State University). It was a prestigious posting for a pastor who was only 25 years old, and it placed him in a position from which he would be pulled to lead the historic Montgomery Bus Boycott in December 1955.

After the boycott's victory in 1956, King and one of his most trusted lieutenants during the boycott, the Rev. Ralph David Abernathy, looked for ways to expand the success in Montgomery to a wider civil rights battlefield. Using the structur-

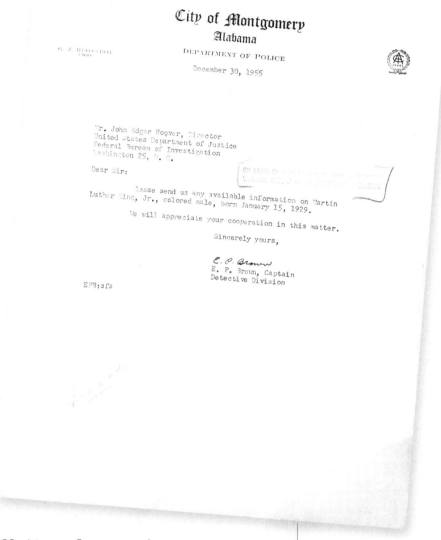

City of Montgomery
Alabama

DEPARTMENT OF POLICE

G. J. RUPPENTHAL
Chief

December 30, 1955

Mr. John Edgar Hoover, Director
United States Department of Justice
Federal Bureau of Investigation
Washington 25, D. C.

Dear Sir:

Please send us any available information on Martin
Luther King, Jr., colored male, born January 15, 1929.

We will appreciate your cooperation in this matter.

Sincerely yours,

E. P. Brown
E. P. Brown, Captain
Detective Division

EPB:sfs

This letter from Montgomery police captain E.P. Brown to FBI Director J. Edgar Hoover asks for background information on the Rev. Martin Luther King Jr. *Courtesy of the Rosa Parks Museum, Troy University*

al model of the Montgomery Improvement Association, which led the bus boycott, King and other Southern ministers created the Southern Christian Leadership Conference in 1957. In 1959, King left Dexter Avenue Baptist Church and Montgomery to become co-pastor with his father at Ebenezer Baptist in Atlanta, which left him more time for civil rights work.

Like the MIA, the SCLC was a largely black organization run by African Americans with the central leadership composed mostly of ministers. But unlike the MIA, which focused on a direct action campaign to right a specific segregation wrong, the SCLC at first focused on increasing black voter registration and participation—important work, but not as exciting as direct confrontation.

The SCLC was drawn into more of an activist role in the early 1960s with the blooming of student protests around the nation exemplified by a wave of sit-in protests at segregated institutions. The forma-

Civil rights leaders Ralph Abernathy and Martin Luther King Jr. (right) worked together for civil rights causes following the boycott.
Don Cravens/Time Life Pictures/Getty Images

tion of the Student Nonviolent Coordinating Committee, with former SCLC administrator Ella Baker as an adviser, gave King's organization some competition as the voice of the Civil Rights Movement on the pages and screens of the national news media.

In 1963, King and the SCLC again focused the world's attention on Alabama as white officials in Birmingham used attack dogs and fire hoses against unarmed black demonstrators. His arrest there (one of 30 arrests during his civil rights campaigns) prompted his writing of the stirring "Letter from Birmingham Jail."

In August 1963, King led a quarter of a million people in the March on Washington that was the occasion of his famous "I Have a Dream" speech from the Lincoln Memorial that cemented his role as the moral voice of the Civil Rights Movement.

In 1963, King was chosen as *Time* magazine's Man of the Year and in 1964, he became, at 35, the youngest man to be honored with the Nobel Peace Prize.

In 1967, King turned his attention to the economic woes suffered by people of all colors by starting the Poor People's Campaign. As part of that effort, he traveled to Memphis in 1968 to support a strike of sanitation workers. It was there, on April 4, 1968, that he was assassinated.

It makes for an enthralling debate to consider whether a man with King's passion for equal rights and his ability to stir those passions in others would have risen to civil rights prominence without being in the right place at the right time when the organ-

The Rev. Martin Luther King Jr., circa 1965.
MPI/Getty Images

izers of the Montgomery Bus Boycott were looking for a compromise leader. A strong case can be made that the writer of the "Letter from Birmingham Jail" and the deliverer of the "I Have a Dream" speech would have emerged as a leader in the Civil Rights Movement, no matter the circumstances.

But when the Montgomery Bus Boycott needed a spokesman, King was there, and there is no denying his lasting and profound impact on the nation.

The Rev. Martin Luther King Jr. emphasizes a point during a sermon shortly after the bus boycott ended. *Montgomery Advertiser files*

Civil rights attorney Arthur Shores and the Rev. Martin Luther King Jr. leave the Montgomery courthouse. *Montgomery Advertiser files*

The Second Front:

B R O W D E R   V .   G A Y L E

Black Montgomerians battled for their freedom using the weapons of shoe leather, unity, nonviolent protest and national publicity, but the leaders of the Montgomery Bus Boycott knew they would have to wage war on a second front to ultimately be victorious. That front came in the form of a federal lawsuit, *Browder v. Gayle*. (Browder was a Montgomery housewife; Gayle the mayor of Montgomery.)

Just days after the beginning of the bus boycott, boycott leaders began discussing the need for a federal lawsuit to challenge city and state bus segregation laws. On January 30, 1956, (the day the Rev. Martin Luther King Jr.'s home was bombed in the early morning hours) the executive board of the Montgomery Improvement Association decided to sue in federal court. Two days later, attorneys Fred Gray and Charles Langford filed the lawsuit on behalf of four female plaintiffs.

Gray recalls in his memoir, *Bus Ride to Justice*, that discussions with MIA leaders about a federal lawsuit began about two weeks after the start of the boycott. Gray quickly began research for the lawsuit, consulting several sympathetic attorneys, including his friend and mentor, Clifford Durr. He also consulted with NAACP legal counsels Robert Carter and Thurgood Marshall, who would later become U.S. solicitor general and a U.S. Supreme Court justice.

Advertiser

Complete CAPITAL EDITION

, February 2, 1956

36 Pages ★

Price 5 Cents

TRAVEL BARRIER CHALLENGED

5 Negroes Attack Segregation Laws In Federal Court

By JOE AZBELL
Advertiser City Editor

Five Montgomery Negro women yesterday filed a suit in the U.S. District Court asking that the courts declare Alabama and Montgomery transportation segregation laws unconstitutional.

The suit, entered in the court at 12:45 p.m. by Attys. Fred Gray and Charles Langford, was filed by Aurelia S. Browder, Susie McDonald, Jeanette Reese, Claudette Colvin by Q. P. Colvin her father, and Mary Louise Smith by Frank Smith, her father.

Named as defendants were Mayor W. A. Gayle, Commissioner Clyde Sellers, Commissioner Frank Parks, individually and as the City Commission, Police Chief G. J. Ruppenthal, the Montgomery City Lines and bus drivers James F. Blake and Robert Cleere.

BULKY DOCUMENT

The bulky court document specifically asks:

1. A final judgment and decree that will declare and define the legal rights of the parties in the controversy.

2. A final judgment and decree that will declare Section 301, Title 48, Code of Alabama and Sections 10 and 11 of the Montgomery City Code, (ordering bus segregation), null and void.

3. A judgment and decree declaring that the acts of the defendants in seeking to compel the plaintiffs and other Negro citizens to use bus facilities by use

...ent is a nation- ...government of- an opportunity Wirephoto

...ade

...OKAY ...TION

...neral Assembly

ONLY DAMAGE TO FENCE

Officials Probing Blast In NAACP Leader's Yard

By STEVE LESHER

An explosive was tossed on the 647 Clinton Ave. last night. No one was injured.

It was the second bombing this week of property owned by Negroes prominent in the boycott of the Montgomery City Lines by Negroes.

Nixon is former state president of the NAACP and current president of the Montgomery Progressive Democratic Assn.

No damage was done to the two-story brick home.

The first bombing was at the

violating the state segregation laws by refusing to yield her seat on a bus to a white person.

The first bombing occurred at King's home at about 10 p.m. on Monday. King was not at home at the time but the house was occupied by his wife, his daughter and a friend. The explosive, which Toxicologist Pruitt said was "one stick of dynamite or a hand grenade," landed on the porch of King's home and broke out several windows, split a porch column and ripped a mailbox from the wall.

Garrett is charged with vote juggling in the 1954 Democratic primaries in an unsuccessful effort to steal the nomination for attorney general from Phenix City vice foe Albert L. Patterson.

He also is charged with murder in the pistol killing of Patterson less than three weeks later. He is yet to be tried on this count also.

'TIME TO BE FRANK'

Mayor Stops Boycott Talk

By JOE AZBELL
Advertiser City Editor

Mayor W. A. Gayle declared yesterday there will be no more discussions with the Negro boycott leaders until they are ready to end the boycott.

The mayor declared in a dynamic statement of his stand on the boycott that the vast majority of whites in Montgomery "do not care whether a Negro ever rides a bus again if it means that the social fabric of our community is to be destroyed so that the Negroes will start riding buses again."

Shortly after the mayor issued his statement, it was announced that the entire City Commission, Mayor Gayle, Commissioner Frank Parks and Commissioner Clyde Sellers, had joined the Montgomery Citizens Council.

Mayor Gayle said that "We have pussyfooted around on this boycott long enough and it has come time to be frank and honest." He added that the Negro leaders have proved "again and again that they will say one thing to a white person and another thing to a Negro about the boycott."

His full text statement follows:
"The City Commission has attempted with sincerity and honesty to end the bus boycott in a businesslike fashion.

"We have held meetings with the Negroes at which proposals were made that would have been accepted by any fair-minded group of people.

"But there seems to be a belief on the part of the Negroes that they have the white people hemmed up in a corner and they are not going to give an inch until they can force the white people of our community to submit to their demands — in fact, swallow all of them.

"The Negro leaders have forced
(See BUS, Page 2A)

Engineer Dies In Train Cab; Autopsy Asked

WILLIAMSON, W. Va., Jan. 23 — The fireman on the "Pocahontas," a Norfolk & Western Railway passenger train which left the rails and plunged into a stream early today, said the big steam locomotive "reared up and started turning over" on a curve.

The engineer was found dead in his cab. At least 32 persons were injured.

The Pocahontas was rolling westward toward Cincinnati with 11 cars when the engine left the tracks 20 miles east of this West Virginia-Kentucky border city.

It plunged down a 40-foot em-

BACKED PORTER

Patterson would have succeeded Garrett, who had backed the vice foe's opponent, Lee Porter of Gadsden. John Patterson, son of the slain crusader, later was elected to the state post without opposition.

The state charged that Garrett, former Russell County Circuit Solicitor Arch Ferrell and Birmingham Atty. Lamar Reid added 600 votes to the total of Patterson's opponent in the Jefferson County tabulation of second primary results.

Ferrell was acquitted at a trial last spring, and Reid threw himself on the mercy of the court. The Birmingham attorney was fined and placed on probation on a reduced charge.

Garrett, Ferrell and former Russell County Chief Deputy Sheriff Albert Fuller were charged with Patterson's murder. Ferrell was acquitted while Fuller was convicted of first degree murder and sentenced to life imprisonment. He has appealed the verdict although he is serving the sentence.

The vote fraud trial date was set by the Jefferson County Solicitor's office.

UNDERGOING TREATMENT

Garrett was undergoing mental treatment in a Texas hospital when the murder indictments were returned in December, 1954. He returned to this state last Oct. 15, declaring that he was innocent and wanted a trial to clear his name. He was released on $12,500 bond.

The state sought to have Garrett committed to Bryce State Hospital for a mental examination. After a lengthy hearing Judge McElroy ruled that to force

Snow Flurries

"We are going to hold our stand. We are not going to be a part of any program that will get Negroes to ride the buses again at the price of the destruction of our heritage and way of life."

–W.A. GAYLE

Gray later wrote that he felt a lawsuit was crucial to bolstering the commitment of those who were conducting the boycott, giving them hope that they could prevail even if city officials stood firm in the face of the boycott itself. Time and events proved Gray's thinking was correct.

It is ironic that in the early days of the boycott, when MIA officials were still negotiating with officials of the city and the bus line, their demands stopped far short of ending segregation on city buses. Instead, those negotiations focused on ending the practices of forcing blacks to stand so that whites could sit, such as in the case of Rosa Parks, or of forcing blacks to leave seats in the front of the black section of a bus so that whites could fill them if the white section was full. The boycott leadership also sought the hiring of some black bus drivers and more courteous treatment of black riders by bus drivers.

"Which," Gray told the *Montgomery Advertiser* several years later, "is not abolishing segregation at all."

If city officials had given in to these modest demands, they would have derailed the boycott and quite likely have caused the fulcrum of the civil rights movement to have shifted to some other city than Montgomery. Indeed, business interests in Montgomery, supported by the *Montgomery Advertiser's* editorial page, supported some form of compromise, as did the majority of the leadership of the MIA.

But city officials, egged on by the militant White Citizens Councils, refused to budge. In the early weeks of the boycott, then-mayor W.A. Gayle declared: "We are going to hold our stand. We are not going to be a part of any program that will get Negroes to ride the buses again at the price of the destruction of our heritage and way of life."

The intransigence on the part of city officials prompted MIA leaders to widen their demands when they went to federal court.

"We concluded that if we were ever going to get anywhere, we would have to go to the federal court," Gray said. "So once we got to that point, we didn't ask the federal court for this [original] point we [had] approached the city with. We filed to end segregation."

The plaintiffs in the case were Aurelia Browder, a housewife; Mrs. Susie McDonald, a black woman in her seventies; Claudette Colvin, the 15-year-old arrested in March 1955 for refusing to give up her bus seat; and Mary Louise Smith, an 18-year-old arrested under similar circumstances in October 1955. The four women had one thing in common: They were black women who had been treated unfairly on city buses because of their race.

The Rosa Parks case was not used as the basis for the federal lawsuit for several reasons. As a criminal statute, it would have to wend its way through the state criminal appeals process

W.A. Gayle, mayor of Montgomery, smiles over telegrams approving action to break up the bus boycott. *Don Cravens/Time Life Pictures/Getty Images*

before a federal appeal could be filed. City and state officials could have delayed a final rendering for years. In addition, it is possible that the only outcome would have been that the conviction of Parks would be vacated, with no lasting impact on bus segregation.

The plaintiffs' attorneys in the *Browder v. Gayle* case were Fred Gray, Charles Langford of Montgomery, Arthur Shores, Peter Hall, Orzell Billingsley Jr. and NAACP counsels Robert Carter and Thurgood Marshall.

A hearing on *Browder v. Gayle* was held in Montgomery on May 11, 1956. The plaintiffs outlined their harsh treatment on city buses before a panel of three federal judges: Appeals Court Judge Richard T. Rives, Montgomery District Judge Frank M. Johnson Jr., and Birmingham District Judge Seybourn H. Lynne.

The attorneys for the black plaintiffs argued that the 1954 Supreme Court ruling in *Brown v. Board of Education of Topeka, Kansas*, applied not only to public education, but to public transportation as well.

But victory for the plaintiffs was far from assured. While Rives had a reputation as a moderate, Lynne was an ardent conservative. The swing vote would come from Johnson, whose appointment to the federal bench had just been confirmed. Johnson would later become known

Lawyers Charles Langford (left), Orzell Billingsley (second from left), Peter Hall (middle), Arthur Shores (second from right) and Fred Gray (right) discuss strategy outside the Montgomery courthouse after a hearing on a motion to end the bus boycott car pool. *Montgomery Advertiser files*

for landmark civil rights rulings, but at the time his legal leanings were largely unknown.

On June 5, the special panel ruled two to one in favor of the black plaintiffs. The Rives majority opinion in which Johnson concurred held that the 1954 Brown ruling, which had overturned the 1896 *Plessy v. Ferguson* "separate but equal" doctrine, applied not only to public schools but to other forms of legalized segregation, including public transportation.

Coretta Scott King (left), the Rev. Ralph D. Abernathy (middle) and the Rev. Martin Luther King Jr. confer outside the courthouse after hearing that the U.S. Supreme Court had ruled in favor of the bus boycotters in *Browder v. Gayle*, clearing the way for the boycott to end.
Montgomery Advertiser files

Still, boycotters could not yet declare victory. The three-judge panel delayed enforcement of its ruling until the city had exhausted its appeals. Because of that delay, the MIA leadership felt it was important for the boycott to continue.

As the federal case wound on, Montgomery Improvement Association attorneys had their hands full staving off attempts in state courts by the city to end the boycott, including the prosecution of boycott leaders for violating the state's anti-boycott law and an effort to enjoin the operation of the MIA's car pool. On November 13, the

day the city got a state court injunction to shut down the car pool, the U.S. Supreme Court ruled in favor of the plaintiffs in the *Browder v. Gayle* case. As soon as new mass meetings could be arranged, several thousand blacks voted to end the boycott when the high court's enforcement order was served. That occurred on December 20, 1956, and black Montgomerians—led by King—returned to the city buses the next day.

The 381-day boycott of Montgomery buses finally had ended. Not only could the black residents of Montgomery now ride city buses as equals, thanks to their efforts so could black citizens throughout the nation.

Attorney Fred Gray uses a diagram of a bus to help illustrate his case against segregated public buses in *Browder v. Gayle*.
Don Cravens/Time Life Pictures/Getty Images

Opposite page: The Rev. Martin Luther King Jr. and Glenn Smiley, an adviser, leave a city bus after a U.S. Supreme Court ruling desegregated Montgomery buses.
Montgomery Advertiser files

Previous page: The Rev. Martin Luther King Jr. (third from left) waits for a bus with the other leaders of the bus boycott at the end of the year-long protest. *Don Cravens/Time Life Pictures/Getty Images*

The media waits outside the Montgomery courthouse during the bus boycott hearings.
Montgomery Advertiser files

IN HIS OWN WORDS:
Fred Gray

F red Gray, who was only 25 years old and fresh out of law school when the Montgomery Bus Boycott began, played a pivotal role in the boycott as well as other civil rights events following it. He represented Rosa Parks in her criminal trial for refusing to give up her seat on a bus, and was the lead attorney on the Browder v. Gayle *case that provided the vehicle for the U.S. Supreme Court to declare segregated public transportation unconstitutional. Gray now practices law in Tuskegee, Alabama. Here are some of his recollections of the Montgomery Bus Boycott and events leading up to it:*

My interest in the boycott started when I lived on the west side of town. I was going to Alabama State [College] and worked as circulation manager for the *Alabama Journal.* Since my district was on the east side, I used the buses from as little as twice a day to as much as six or eight times a day. While I never had an altercation myself on the bus—in fact, I have had very few altercations at all because I try to avoid those situations—I was very concerned about how African Americans were treated on buses.

I did see many incidents where black people were asked to get up and give their seats to white people, particularly if the bus was pretty much full of white people. The blacks would get on in the front of the bus, pay their fare and then get off and walk to the back door to get on. In a few instances I saw drivers leave before they could get back on, although I don't think they did it intentionally.

The bus situation and how people were treated was a grave concern of mine, and it had something to do later on with my decision to become a lawyer. I had not planned to be a lawyer. In fact, I did not even know a lawyer nor what lawyers did.

Jo Ann Robinson, who later became a very important movement figure doing more work behind the scenes than out front, had a real personal interest in the bus situation. In 1948 she was an instructor at Alabama State and during a school break she got on a bus and sat down about middle ways—it wasn't crowded—but she just got a mean bus driver who wanted her to sit farther back. She became very indignant about it and got off the bus. She started keeping a record of incidents that happened on the buses.

Then in 1954 or '55 she became president of the Women's Political Council, which was a group of African-American professional women, mostly teachers in and around Alabama State and in the public school system. They were working on various civic projects, including encouraging people to vote, and she got them to adopt the business of documenting the events that occurred on the buses.

On March 2, 1955, I started representing Claudette Colvin. Claudette was a 15-year-old young lady who lived on Dixie Court and she went to Booker Washington High School. She used the public transportation system and transferred in downtown Montgomery to go to and from school. On this particular day she had boarded the bus, gone a couple of stops, and then when it got to Commerce and Bibb, the bus driver, who was a white man, asked her to get up, and Claudette just didn't get up. She

---

An ordained minister before he became an attorney, Fred D. Gray served as minister of the Newtown Church of Christ on Ferguson Street in Montgomery from 1957-1973. This photo was taken around the time of the bus boycott.
Don Cravens/Time Life Pictures/Getty Images

didn't say anything, she just didn't move. The police came and asked her to move and she still wouldn't move. She literally was dragged off the bus and arrested, and I was called to represent her.

She had been included in a group of young ladies who were working with Mrs. Rosa Parks in connection with the NAACP youth group. When I opened my office, Mr. [E.D.] Nixon had encouraged me to start a political group (The Young Alabama Democrats) to get teenagers and young college students and their parents registered to vote.

A young lady, Annie Larkins, who was a friend of Claudette's, was also on the bus and witnessed Claudette's case. Those youngsters were a part of that political group and also a part of Mrs. Parks's youth group. But in Claudette's case, I think she just decided on her own to do whatever she was going to do. She didn't know what in the world was going to happen to her.

I don't mean to take anything away from Mrs. Parks, but Claudette gave to all of us the moral courage to do what we later did. I know she did it for me and for Jo Ann Robinson.

In those days if you were a person of color your chances of getting justice were not very good. It was difficult to get a lawyer, because they were all white lawyers. We didn't have any black lawyers then. The white lawyers were afraid that if they took a case like that it would interrupt their other cases, so there were not many lawyers who would do it. So I made a secret commitment that I was going to not only be a preacher, but that I was going to be a lawyer. I was even going to apply to the University of Alabama.

In those days Alabama offered a portion of the tuition, room and board if [black students] would go to another school rather than go to the University of Alabama. So I took advantage of that. I decided I was going to go away, take the bar exam and return to destroy everything segregated I could find.

I didn't tell anybody—not even my mother—that I was applying for law school until I was accepted. After I got an acceptance letter from Case Western University in Cleveland, I just politely eased the letter to her at the dinner table one day and she said, "Well, Mr. Smarty, now that you

have been accepted, where are you going to get the money from?"

I felt that if there was just one black lawyer, it would make a difference. When I went to law school, every paper I wrote was on Alabama law.

During the early years I didn't handle a case alone. I always had another lawyer who was more experienced than I was to work with.

During my senior year one of my professors suggested that I stay in Cleveland, because he didn't think I would have much of an opportunity if I went back home. He even suggested some good black law firms that I might find employment with. I thanked him, but I explained to him that the only reason I went there to law school was to return to Alabama to practice. He then advised me that if I did go back, not to be afraid to share a fee with a lawyer who had more experience. As things developed, I got the very best help that I could get because I realized that the other side was going to have the very best lawyers Alabama had, and if we were going to compete, we were going to have to prepare all of our cases as if we were going to the Supreme Court. So that was my motivating factor.

Mrs. Parks would come from her office in Montgomery Fair to my office across the street, and we would have lunch together. We met and talked that day (December 1, 1955, the day of her arrest) and I was probably the last person she talked to before she was arrested. She left about 1 p.m., and I had to go out of town that afternoon. When I got back I had a message from her telling me that she had been arrested. She indicated that she wanted me to come by, and I went and talked to her and she told me what had taken place. She said her trial was set for Monday and this was on a Thursday. I told her I would be glad to represent her.

When I left her I went to E.D. Nixon's and talked to him, because we all had some real concerns about the buses and all matters concerning civil rights. After talking to him I felt that he was ready for us to move forward to do whatever we had to do. I then left his house and went over to Jo Ann Robinson's. We talked for the next five or six hours, and really, in her living room, made the plans and road map about what we thought needed to happen.

This is a May 1966 photo of attorney Fred D. Gray campaigning in Eufaula, Alabama, for the Alabama legislature. *AP/WWP*

Mrs. Robinson was teaching at Alabama State, and if the power structure knew that she was advocating and working toward integrating anything she would have been fired immediately. She was later fired anyway. She really did not want anybody to find out what she did, and I had just finished law school and I had to be very careful or I knew I would find myself disbarred before I was ever barred. We planted the seeds and communicated with others who ultimately made the decisions.

Mrs. Robinson played a very pivotal role, as I did, because we sat there and analyzed what really needed to happen based on the experience we had with Claudette Colvin's case. We concluded that if we were ever to do anything to solve the bus problem, now was the time to do it. The question was how do you do it?

These were some of the things we considered: First, the group of people who had their finger on more people than any others in our communities were the black preachers, so we had to get help from the black preachers.

Second, we knew we had basically two black leaders in the community at that time. E.D. Nixon was not an educated man, but he had good common sense and had been president of the state conference of the NAACP, and if anybody ever had any kind of problem they would go to E.D. Nixon, and he would do what he could. He had contacts with lawyers who would handle these kind of cases.

Attorney Fred D. Gray (left), the Rev. Ralph D. Abernathy (center), and the Rev. Robert S. Graetz discuss a proposed bus boycott settlement on February 21, 1956. *AP/WWP*

On the other hand, we had Rufus Lewis, who was educated, a former coach at Alabama State, a businessman, his wife was the co-owner of the largest funeral home in town, and he was interested only in the political aspect—the Board of Registration and getting people elected. If you had any other kind of problem you did not need to talk to Rufus Lewis, because he wasn't interested. He was the owner of a club on the west side of town named the Citizens Club, and in order to get in the Citizens Club you had to be a registered voter.

So we knew that we needed those two persons and we also recognized that people got hung up over personalities, so we knew we would need somebody to serve as spokesman for the group. The logical person would have been one of the two folks who had been doing something in the area of civil rights, but we also felt that if either of them was selected it would mean we might lose someone else's support, so I asked Jo Ann who she thought would make a good spokesman.

She suggested her pastor, Dr. King (Martin Luther King Jr.). I had met Dr. King, but I did not know him like she knew him, but she highly recom-

mended him. She said he was articulate, had only been here a short period of time. He had not been involved in any civil rights activities, he was well thought of, he was young, he was energetic. She said he would be the ideal spokesman, and then we could come up with good supporting roles for these other persons, because we would need money for gas and to transport these folks because they had to go to work. If we didn't come up with a plan for them it was just not going to work.

Then, of course, there was the legal aspect. I was available to do that. So what we concluded was that E.D. Nixon was a member of the union that A. Philip Randolph was the president of and he knew Nixon. We felt that if the group were to select Nixon as the treasurer, he could get Randolph to raise some money nationally for the movement, and that made sense.

The other key part of this was transportation, and I said Rufus Lewis was the ideal person for that because his wife was co-owner of the funeral home. They had automobiles and they had contacts with other funeral homes that had automobiles. So we suggested him for chairman of the transportation committee.

We then assigned ourselves responsibilities. Certain people would contact certain persons and suggest certain things, and when the organizational meeting was held in Mt. Zion AME Zion Church, Dr. King was elected as the spokesman even though he wasn't at the meeting, E.D. Nixon was selected as treasurer, Rufus Lewis was selected as chairman of transportation, and I was selected as lawyer—and the rest is history.

This was decided at a meeting on Monday after the trial. We had some leaflets made up calling for a boycott, and then we had a meeting of all the preachers and leaders at Dexter. That was really the first official meeting. Then we had the trial.

We were trying to keep it out of the press, but Nixon had the support of Joe Azbell, and he leaked the story to Joe, which was probably the best thing that could have happened, because then it ended as front-page news in the paper on Sunday saying that we were planning a boycott.

I was hoping that they would charge Rosa with violation of the segregation ordinance but they were too smart to do that. Instead they charged her with disorderly conduct. That, from the community's point of view was good, because everybody knew that Mrs. Parks wouldn't be disorderly toward anybody. She didn't have that kind of personality, so to even charge her with that was just out of the question. The most we could get out of Mrs. Parks's case was to have her found not guilty. (She was found guilty and fined $14.)

We still had the city ordinances and state laws, so I had been working on a complaint ever since Claudette's days, but I had to be sure that I had the community with me; I could not run out there by myself. I knew that I had only been out of school a short period of time, and [Birmingham attorney] Arthur Shores had been working on these types of cases for years, so I asked him to become involved in it. At the time, Peter Hall and Orzell Billingsley were working out of Arthur's office, so that's how they got involved.

In addition to that, I realized, too, that the case was going to go all the way to the Supreme Court eventually, so I immediately got the NAACP involved. Robert Carter was the assistant general counselor then and Thurgood Marshall and within two weeks after the bus boycott started, I went to New York to talk to them. This was in early December. And I had taken with me a copy of my draft of the complaint for their review. We worked on it all day, and they told me they would give me legal assistance. That was the beginning of my relationship with the NAACP that has lasted all these years.

I was also working on a lawsuit to integrate the buses, because at some point the boycott was going to end and we would go back to whatever normalcy was, so the whole thing was that we would stay off the buses until we could do it on an integrated basis. Then there was the business of the day-to-day operation, because once we got started the police were watching us every day and charging us with all kinds of traffic violations. The question came up as to what organization was going to sponsor it, and I suggested to them that we not use any of the existing organizations because if we had anything they would come after you. The best thing to do was to create a new organization that had nothing so they could not lose anything and let it be the vehicle.

They came up with the name Montgomery Improvement Association. Six months later Judge Jones issued his temporary restraining order enjoining the NAACP from doing business in the state so if they had been the organizer of the boycott we would have had a problem.

The Browder v. Gayle *lawsuit brought by Fred Gray and his legal team was successful in overturning the state and local bus segregation laws, but that was not the end of Gray's involvement in the Civil Rights Movement. He later represented Freedom Riders, Selma-to-Montgomery civil rights marchers, and the victims of the infamous Tuskegee Syphilis Study. He was the first African American to serve as president of the Alabama Bar Association. He still practices law in Tuskegee, where he is working to create the Tuskegee Human and Civil Rights Multicultural Center.*

The White Community

O ne of the strongest weapons used by the black citizens of Montgomery to stage the Montgomery Bus Boycott was unity. While the black community in Montgomery presented a united front in support of the Montgomery Bus Boycott, nothing approaching that sort of unity existed in the white community to oppose it.

This is not to say that many whites openly supported the boycott; the majority either opposed it or at least acquiesced to the city's official opposition. Many in the business community, led by an economic development group called the Men of Montgomery, initially worked for a compromise, although they were eventually shouted down by more reactionary voices, including those affiliated with the openly racist White Citizens Council.

But a handful of whites played key roles in the boycott, and a few courageous whites raised their voices to support fairer treatment for blacks. In almost every case, those whites who spoke out to defend blacks suffered retaliation ranging from outright violence to loss of business to social ostracism.

For instance, the Rev. Robert Graetz, who led the all-black congregation at Trinity Lutheran Church on Cleveland Avenue (now appropriately renamed Rosa L. Parks Avenue), was the only white member of the board of the Montgomery Improvement Association. Graetz and his wife,

Jeannie, received almost routine anonymous threats of violence, and their home was bombed twice.

In his book, *A White Preacher's Memoir: The Montgomery Bus Boycott,* Graetz wrote of sugar being placed in the gasoline tank of his car. When he had it towed to be repaired, a white mechanic called him aside and, asking for his warning to be confidential, told him that his tires had been cut on the inside so that the cuts wouldn't show. The cuts didn't go all the way through, causing Graetz to assume that the vandals meant for the tires to blow out after they heated up while he was driving. When Graetz discussed the damage with his insurance agency, the agent warned him that if he made the claim his insurance would likely be canceled. He paid for the damage from his own pocket, but his insurance was canceled anyway.

Also chief among the Montgomery whites who lent their support to the boycott efforts were attorney Clifford Durr and his wife, Virginia, who helped to bail Rosa Parks out of jail after her arrest. Even though he remained behind the scenes in helping with boycott-related legal work, Clifford Durr saw his law practice suffer, and Virginia Durr felt she was socially ostracized.

Shortly after the U.S. Supreme Court struck down Alabama's bus segregation laws, Virginia Durr wrote to a friend about their treatment by other whites: "We are no more unpopular than we

The Rev. Robert Graetz, a Lutheran minister who was the only white Montgomery Improvement Association board member, speaks at a mass meeting during the bus boycott. *Montgomery Advertiser files*

have been, and actually we are not so unpopular personally as we are 'suspect' as being heretics. We are no longer members of the tribe, and there are penalties attached to that…mostly economic ones, but so far we survive, and that is a real triumph."

One of the ironies of the Montgomery Bus Boycott is that a movement so closely affiliated with black churches received so little support from white ministers in the community (although many national church organizations supported the boycott and even contributed funds). Author Donald E. Collins sheds light on one reason why in his book on the Methodist Church's role in the Civil Rights Movement in Alabama, wonderfully

titled *When the Church Bell Rang Racist.*

Collins tells of the Rev. Ray Whatley, minister of St. Mark Methodist Church and president of the Montgomery chapter of the Alabama Council on Human Relations. After Whatley wrote a letter to the mayor supporting a settlement with the boycott organizers, officials of his church requested that he be reassigned. The Methodist bishop moved Whatley to the small

> "We are no longer members of the tribe, and there are penalties attached to that...mostly economic ones, but so far we survive, and that is a real triumph."
>
> –VIRGINIA DURR, from *Freedom Writer: Virginia Foster Durr, Letters from the Civil Rights Years*

Alabama town of Linden, but his troubles followed him. Some members of his Linden congregation withdrew financial support from the church and demanded he be moved again. The bishop complied after a year.

Police identified another white Methodist minister, the Rev. Joe Neal Blair, as he attended one of the mass meetings in a black church during the bus boycott. Forty years later, Blair told his Sunday school class at Dalraida United Methodist Church in Montgomery that for at least two decades after the boycott, officials of new churches to which he was assigned would quiz him about that incident and his later attempts to bring the races together.

One of the more poignant stories arising out of the boycott involved a Montgomery librarian, Juliette Morgan. Long before the Montgomery Bus Boycott, this quiet librarian from one of Montgomery's socially prominent families had written letters to the editor of the *Montgomery Advertiser* criticizing the treatment of blacks. She even started a mini-bus boycott of her own,

pulling the stop cord and leaving buses herself when she saw a black person abused by a bus driver in some way. Until the bus boycott began in December 1955, other whites usually just laughed at her actions and her letters.

But on December 12, just a week after the boycott started, Morgan again wrote the *Advertiser*, this time comparing the Montgomery Bus Boycott to the movement in India inspired by Mohandas Gandhi. This stand aroused reactionary whites, who called for her firing from the city library. Library officials refused to fire her, but asked that she stop writing letters to the editor. She agreed, but reneged by agreeing to let the *Tuscaloosa News* publish a letter in 1957 that renewed calls for her firing. Again library officials stood behind her, but White Citizens Council members organized a boycott of the library. A cross was burned in her yard. The mayor threatened to eliminate her job.

On July 15, 1957, this librarian later described by the Rev. Martin Luther King Jr. as "sensitive and frail," resigned from the library and

The Rev. Ralph D. Abernathy (left), the Rev. Robert S. Graetz (center), and the Rev. Martin Luther King Jr., talk outside the witness room during the post-boycott bombing trial on May 28, 1957. The homes and churches of several people involved in the boy-cott were bombed soon after the buses were ordered integrated. *AP/WWP*

committed suicide by taking sleeping pills.

But her 1955 letter to the *Advertiser* helped show the community that not all whites were unsympathetic to the Montgomery Bus Boycott. She compared the boycott to Gandhi's "Salt March" to the sea, and wrote:

"One feels that history is being made in Montgomery these days, the most important in her career. It is hard to imagine a soul so dead, a heart so hard, a vision so blinded and provincial as not to be moved with admiration at the quiet dignity, discipline, and dedication with which the Negroes have conducted their boycott…

"I am all for law and order, the protection of person and property against violence, but I believe the Constitution and Supreme Court of the United States constitute the supreme law of the land. I find it ironical to hear men in authori-

Virginia Durr (center) attends a mass meeting the summer after the bus boycott ended. Virginia Durr was a friend to Rosa Parks, and her husband, attorney Clifford Durr, aided boycott attorneys behind the scenes. *Montgomery Advertiser files*

ty who are openly flouting this law speak piously of law enforcement.

"I also find it hard to work up sympathy for the bus company. I have ridden the buses of Montgomery ever since they have been running. I have ridden them from once to four times a day for the past 14 years until this October…I have heard some bus drivers use the tone and manners of mule drivers in their treatment of Negro passengers. (Incidentally Negroes pay full fare for fourth-class treatment.) Three times I've gotten off the bus because I could not countenance treatment of Negroes. I should have gotten off on several other occasions. Twice I have heard a certain driver with high seniority mutter quite audibly, "Black ape." I could not tell whether the Negro heard or not, but I did and felt insulted…

"Instead of acting like sullen adolescents whose attitude is 'Make me,' we ought to be working out plans to span the gap—between segregation and integration to extend public services— schools, libraries, parks—and transportation to Negro citizens. Ralph McGill's (the editor of the

Atlanta Constitution) is the best advice I've heard: 'Segregation is on its way out, and he who tries to tell the people otherwise does them great disservice. The problem of the future is how to live with the change.'"

Glenn Smiley of the Fellowship of Reconciliation speaks with an unidentified woman. Smiley worked behind the scenes to help the Rev. Martin Luther King Jr. develop bus boycott strategies, especially the policy of nonviolence. *Montgomery Advertiser files*

IN HIS OWN WORDS:
Robert S. Graetz

When white Lutheran minister Robert S. Graetz and his wife, Jeannie, accepted a call to serve an all-black church in Montgomery, Alabama, in 1955, little did they know that they would soon become immersed in one of the pivotal civil rights events of the decade. The Rev. Graetz became a member of the board of the Montgomery Improvement Association, which sponsored the Montgomery Bus Boycott.

When word spread that a white minister was playing a key role in the boycott, he and his family became a target for white racists. They and their children were the targets of frequent threats, and eventually their home was bombed.

The Rev. Graetz tells part of his story in his own words:

———————

I had graduated from the seminary in Columbus, Ohio, early June of 1955, and we came to Montgomery when I got a call to serve Trinity Lutheran Church. Their pastor left to serve another church during my senior year and they knew my reputation, having already served in black communities, and we didn't have enough black pastors at that time because the Lutheran Church required college and seminary. The schools for blacks both in the North and South at that time were so miserable it was very difficult for black students to go to those terrible schools and then make it in college and seminary, so they needed all the white pastors who were available to serve black congregations. That's how I got to be here serving a black congregation.

I think there were about 200 members altogether at Trinity, and in the Lutheran Church that includes babies.

Before the bus boycott started, it was a very normal pastorate. We had confirmation classes, we had baptisms, weddings, funerals, meetings. I spent a great deal of time visiting in the homes, and I was busy getting acquainted with other pastors, particularly black pastors.

There was a white Lutheran congregation here. The black congregation was part of what was then called the American Lutheran Church, and the white congregation was part of what was called the United Evangelical Church, so they were different church bodies, but all Lutheran. The pastor at that time was Russell Boggs, who became a good friend and strong supporter. During the bus boycott he was a very courageous man. In fact, when he left that congregation he left to go into the paratroopers. He continued to show his courage.

We got word of the boycott on December 2, the day after Mrs. Parks was arrested. There was another black Lutheran congregation in town, by the way, and that was a part of the Lutheran Church, Missouri Synod. It was just getting started; it was a mission congregation, and the pastor there was a dear friend of ours. He called us and told us that somebody had been arrested and there was supposed to be a boycott, so that was the first realization that we had, but he didn't know who it was. So I called another dear friend, Mrs. Rosa Parks, to ask her what was going on, and of course she told us.

On Sunday morning I announced to the congregation that they should stay off the buses on Monday and that I would be out with my car driving my people to work. We had then made a commitment to be a part of it for the duration.

I got to as many mass meetings as I could, but we had other commitments at the church that we also had to take care of. I probably got to two-thirds of them; at least half. We just had to keep up with both the church and the movement at the same time.

The only white member of the MIA board was Robert S. Graetz, a Lutheran minister who helped lead the Montgomery Bus Boycott, shown here with the Rev. Martin Luther King Jr. *Montgomery Advertiser files*

Everyday life changed rather quickly after the boycott began. At first it changed in that I was out driving my car several hours a day, which cut into the time that was available for other things. We had to really work hard to get our normal chores taken care of. After the word went out in the *Montgomery Advertiser,* when Tom Johnson wrote an article about my involvement in the boycott in January, our days were interrupted by nasty phone calls and all sorts of other things. But all of us who were involved, particularly those in leadership, had to keep up with the normal routine of things.

The lay people had to keep up with their regular jobs of 40 hours a week, and the pastors had to make sure we were still serving our congregations in addition to all the other things—endless meetings, entertaining visitors, etc.

We had a constant flow of visitors to our house during that whole time. There were some really notable visitors. One was a member of the Indian Parliament who came just to see what was going on since our movement was modeled after Mohandas Gandhi.

And there were reporters from all over the world. I remember that there was a church reporter from Denmark who promised me he would send me what he wrote after he got back. Many people promised the same thing, and none of them ever sent anything back, but this man sent back his article. Of course it was in Danish, so it didn't help much.

When we arrived, our children were one and two years old. We added three more while we were here and left at the end of 1958 with five children. Then we had two more after we left here.

There was a major concern for their safety. We realized that we had the right to endanger our own lives, but we really struggled with whether we had the right to endanger their lives. People who lived not too far from us and could actually see the front of our house would call us and say something about where the children were, so we knew we were under observation. That was difficult. We finally decided that God had brought us here, and we couldn't take care of them but God would, and so we went about our business.

> The Rev. Robert S. Graetz talks with his parishioners outside the church.
> *Don Cravens/Time Life Pictures/Getty Images*

"We finally decided that God had brought us here, and we couldn't take care of [our children] but God would, and so we went about our business."

–ROBERT S. GRAETZ

We played games with them, particularly after the first bomb hit our house. We had a couch which sat away from the wall, and we told them that if we ever said, "Go hide," they were to go hide behind the couch. We thought that if we heard something we would get them to go hide and they would be safe before the bomb went off. The first bomb was in August 1956, so that would be eight months after the boycott started.

Shortly after the article appeared in the *Advertiser*, when the threatening phone calls and letters started, we knew there was danger involved. They slashed our tires in such a way that they would not deflate immediately, but would be deflated when I was on the road someplace. They put sugar in the gas tank and threw things at the house.

Dr. King used to talk about the reality that some of us were going to die, and that if any of us were afraid to die we really shouldn't be there. Everybody assumed that Dr. King was the primary target and that I was high on the list since I was the only white person on the Montgomery Improvement Association board.

The first bombing was in August 1956. They decided that it was three or four sticks of dynamite and it was near the road. It did substantial damage to the house but no major structural damage. On January 10, 1957, well after the boycott was over and the buses were running again, they bombed four churches and two houses and that was the night that the large bomb did not go off. There were some large bombs that were thrown at some of the churches that caused so much damage they had to be torn down, but the only other bomb that was large enough to kill people was found on the porch of Dr. King's house, but it did not go off.

The group that actually instigated the boycott was not the ministers. It was the Women's Political Council headed by Professor Jo Ann Robinson. The leadership of the Montgomery Improvement Association was not organized until after the boycott was set to go.

Once it began, the people who were best able to serve as leaders were the ministers, because they were the most protected from being harmed by the community, since their salaries were paid by their own congregations. White people didn't hire them and couldn't fire them, so that was the group best able to step in and provide that kind of leadership. The lay people who were on the board tended to be business people in the black community, like Rufus Lewis, who was an undertaker.

I am convinced that the ministers played a key role in the whole program. Keep in mind that in the black community there were no major community programs or centers outside of the church. Virtually all of the life of the community centered in the churches, and the natural leaders of the churches, of course, were the ministers. So when the ministers were standing up and taking positions of leadership, you had the congregations following them, which was virtually all of the black population.

The Women's Political Council, which was all women, was organized because the League of

Women Voters refused to allow black women to join, so they were organizing their own league just with a different name.

This was a group that was raring to go. They were trying to find some way to improve the life of the black people in Montgomery. They had actually warned the bus drivers that if they didn't stop being vicious to their passengers, they would boycott their buses.

We got an amazing amount of support from white pastors. The ones who spoke out openly didn't last long. There were a lot of Methodist pastors who would speak out, and when it came time for the district conference, the congregation would talk to the district superintendent and tell him not to send that man back.

Robert Hughes was the director of the Alabama Council of Human Relations, so he was immune to being fired by the congregation. There was also an Episcopal rector, Tom Thrasher, who was very outspoken as well and ultimately he lost his position, too, but he hung on a lot longer than some of the others.

Some of the rabbis were saying some things, but they were more protected because the Jewish congregations were more isolated in terms of the overall community, and many people were not aware of what was being said.

The white Baptist pastors were among the worst in preaching segregation and supporting the discriminatory policies of the community.

There were a number of white pastors who felt that they dared not speak out because they knew they would be gone quickly. But they wanted to try to accomplish some things behind the scenes, and we organized a state pastors association, black and white, and had representatives from most of the cities in Alabama. Here in Montgomery we had a pretty strong group. We had regular meetings all around the state, and the white pastors were working as much as they could to try to bring about change and to try to assist what was happening in the black community, even though they felt that they could not speak out openly because they felt that that was committing suicide.

Very early in the boycott I mailed a letter to all of the ministers in the white ministerial association, including rabbis as well as Christian pastors,

encouraging them to find out what was really going on in the boycott and to learn what the black people in Montgomery were really asking for, because in the beginning there was so much confusion. I got almost no response at all, because the ones who would have been supportive were afraid that coming to a meeting like that would blow their cover and they would be out of there, and the ones who were opposed were certainly not going to attend such a meeting.

Later when I heard pastors proclaiming segregation in what I thought was such a vile way, my disappointment turned to grief. I thought these were the people who should be leading us and bringing us together instead of separating people.

Sadly, Mrs. Parks had very little to do with the boycott. Once it was past the beginning, she faded into the background. She lost her job, as did her husband. They had to go to Detroit to be with her brother. She left around 1957 or 1958.

There were some whites who were extremely important, and the first ones who come to mind are Clifford and Virginia Durr. They returned to Montgomery after he was no longer in the federal administration. He was planning to practice law here, but his practice never really got very far, because they were known to be liberals and the people simply wouldn't go to him for their legal things. But they hung on and continued to be outspoken, continued to befriend black and white people and to do everything they could, very openly, here in Montgomery. They were courageous people.

There were also several Jewish families who were involved. Percentage-wise we got more support from the Jewish community than from the gentile community. I have always believed it was because the Jews understood oppression, and so when they saw other oppressed groups they could feel for what was going on there. They could sense that something was wrong here, but many of them were afraid to be known, particularly business people. They could never let their involvement be open, because their business could just be wiped out overnight. Every time we see certain Jewish people, they apologize for not having been involved—for at least not being more open...

Probably the most popular things for the Klan types to do was to harass people, particularly with phone calls. The mayor and other white leaders just blasted white women who picked up their maids at shopping centers. They said they were destroying the fabric of society and that they were a part of the Negro movement when they did that. The Klan types actually followed these people and got their license numbers, tracked down who they were and published lists of their names and phone numbers. These women would then get phone calls in the middle of the night.

The mayor said the rides had to stop. One courageous housewife said that if the mayor wants to come in here and clean my house, feed my children, and do my laundry, that's fine, but otherwise I need my Annie. There were a good many who continued to do that.

Anywhere it was possible, there was pressure to fire the blacks who continued to work. They would ask the maids if they were part of the movement, and the maids would deny it. A lot of blacks were fired and harassed.

There were two keys to the boycott's success. One was the role of love and nonviolence in Montgomery. Everything that grew out of what

happened in Montgomery was influenced by that spirit. I am convinced that that is one reason Montgomery was able to withstand the other changes that came along.

The other key: This was the first time that a substantial number of black people were able to take their own action, where they stood together and did not falter, ultimately winning a substantial victory. What that did for the black people in this country was simply incalculable.

The Rev. King's major contribution was the spirit of love and nonviolence he brought to the cause. He had studied Gandhi; he knew the importance of standing up against oppression, yet doing it in a nonviolent manner.

A key time in that development in the community was January 30, 1956, when his house was bombed the first time. That night there was a crowd that gathered in the street around his house that was going to seek vengeance. They had weapons and were ready to start killing some white people.

Dr. King came out on his porch, quieted the crowd and reminded them that this was a movement based on peace, love, and nonviolence. He said in effect, "We don't act like they do. They may treat us violently, but we are not going to do that." He asked the people to go home peacefully, and they did.

From that point on, the message continued week after week after week until it became totally a part of the psyche of the black people of Montgomery. Anybody who wanted to be violent was really going against the grain and realized that they were not supported by the movement here. So that was his major contribution.

> ## "We don't act like they do. They may treat us violently, but we are not going to do that."
>
> —MARTIN LUTHER KING JR.

In addition to that, of course, one of the things that allowed him to be heard so well was that he was a brilliant man, highly intellectual, but also a masterful orator and he could speak in language that would lift people up to a different level. Poor people, uneducated people, would sit there and would hear him as if he was saying, "You are good enough to understand what I am talking about." He could also say it in a way that they did understand. He really elevated them and helped to create within the masses of black people an aura of value and worth and personhood that they had not experienced before. I think that was the genius of his contribution.

Robert and Jeannie Graetz returned to live in Montgomery throughout the 50th anniversary of the Montgomery Bus Boycott to lecture and take part in commemorative ceremonies. After his retirement they continued to work for civil rights and often led pilgrimages of students to Montgomery to study the civil rights movement. He is the author of A White Preacher's Memoir: The Montgomery Bus Boycott.

The Rev. Robert S. Graetz and his wife, Jeannie, visit the Rosa Parks Museum at Troy University.
Mickey Welsh/Advertiser Staff

A PROFILE:
The Durrs

Of the relative handful of white Montgomerians who openly supported the bus boycott, Clifford and Virginia Durr are among the best remembered 50 years later. Their efforts have been noted in books, articles, and oral histories, and in 2005 a historic marker was placed at their former residence in Montgomery.

Their backgrounds were not the sort that might have been expected to produce such dedicated advocates of justice and civil liberties.

Clifford Durr was born in 1899 into a well-established Montgomery family. He attended the Starke University School for Boys, for decades the city's leading private school. Although his marks were excellent, he did not look back fondly on his days there, biographer John Salmond wrote in *The Conscience of a Lawyer*.

Durr enrolled in the University of Alabama in 1915 and completed his degree in 1919, despite several months away from school for military training that he hoped would lead to service in France in World War I. The war ended before Durr had the chance to serve.

Durr was awarded a Rhodes scholarship in 1919 and sailed for Oxford in January 1920. Although he wrote to family members that he found the English "as sociable as an iceberg," his studies in law formed the foundation of a distinguished legal career, according to Salmond.

Virginia Foster Durr was the daughter of a Presbyterian minister who was forced from the church for his refusal to state an absolute belief in the literal truth of Scripture. Throughout her long life, she would struggle with—and ceaselessly challenge—the institutional church.

Her racial sensitivities got a pivotal test when she enrolled in Wellesley College in 1921. At the Massachusetts college, she found herself expected to eat at the same table as blacks, a shock to a young Southern woman of her time and upbringing.

Her family's finances would not allow her to complete her education at Wellesley and she left after her sophomore year. She met Clifford Durr after returning to Alabama. For all their stark differences in temperament, it would prove to be a splendid match that would last for nearly 50 years. The English writer Jessica Mitford, their longtime friend, once described them as "intertwined like two trees of utterly different species."

In the years after their 1926 wedding, Clifford Durr built a legal practice that would have positioned them for a comfortable lifestyle. In 1933, however, he left the Birmingham law firm in which he was a partner and went to work for a federal agency—the Reconstruction Finance Corporation—that was being expanded under the New Deal programs of the new president, Franklin Delano Roosevelt.

Later, Durr was named to the Federal Communications Commission, where he was a leading advocate of public broadcasting.

During their Washington years, Virginia Durr had become increasingly politically active. In one notable example, she worked for years on a campaign to end the poll tax.

By the time the Durrs returned to Alabama where he started a law practice, the rumblings and racial tensions that would eventually spawn the

Clifford Durr provided counsel to the leaders of the bus boycott, especially to attorney Fred Gray.
Courtesy of Walter Lyon

civil rights movement were palpable. Clifford Durr would soon become part of a case that would far outweigh the significance of any he had previously handled in his Montgomery practice.

The story of Rosa Parks is told elsewhere in this book. However, the role of Clifford and Virginia Durr in that historic case is worth noting. The Durrs accompanied E.D. Nixon to the Montgomery jail to arrange bail after Parks was arrested.

Virginia Durr and Rosa Parks were friends even before the arrest of Parks. Durr arranged a scholarship for Parks to attend a seminar at the Highlander Folk School in Tennessee in the summer of 1955, just a few months before her arrest.

Virginia Durr was an inveterate letter writer who had many of her letters collected in *Freedom Writer: Virginia Foster Durr, Letters from the Civil Rights Years*. In one of those letters, she wrote to friends at Highlander of the effects of the school on Parks: "When she came back she felt so liberated, and then as time went on she said the discrimination got worse and worse to bear after having, for the first time in her life, been free of it at Highlander. I am sure that had a lot to do with her daring to risk arrest as she is naturally a very quiet and retiring person although she has a fierce sense of pride and is, in my opinion, a really noble woman."

Clifford Durr would provide invaluable advice to the young lawyer who represented Parks, Fred Gray. He did so quietly and behind the scenes, with no wish for credit for, or even public association with, the Parks case. Years later, Gray would recall in his memoir that without Durr's work, "it would have been almost impossible for the movement to have survived."

Virginia Durr often typed the legal briefs that were filed in the case. "To be able to help just a little has changed my entire point of view," she wrote to a friend.

It soon became evident that the bus boycott was no minor statement of protest, but was a seri-

> "I am sure that had a lot to do with her [Rosa Parks] daring to risk arrest as she is naturally a very quiet and retiring person although she has a fierce sense of pride and is, in my opinion, a really noble woman."
>
> –VIRGINIA DURR

Virginia Durr (left) and Rosa Parks continued their friendship after the boycott and often made appearances together in support of civil rights.
Montgomery Advertiser files

> # "To be able to help just a little has changed my entire point of view."
>
> ## –VIRGINIA DURR

ous effort undertaken by people prepared to make it last as long as necessary.

"The bus boycott still goes on and on," Virginia Durr wrote to Jessica Mitford in 1956, noting that black Montgomerians "have kept it up in spite of rain, cold, and distance."

The Durrs' views on racial equality and civil rights, which were well known before the boycott and were only underscored during it, kept them ostracized from much of Montgomery's social life and also assured that Clifford Durr's law practice would not be profitable. As Virginia Durr often noted years later, her husband had clients; they were simply clients who couldn't afford to pay him anything.

In a letter to a family friend after the U.S. Supreme Court in November 1956 upheld the ruling in *Browder v. Gayle* that segregation on public transportation was unconstitutional, Virginia Durr wrote that they were "no more unpopular than we have been."

"We are no longer members of the tribe," she wrote, "and there are penalties attached to that as you know, mostly economic ones, but so far we survive and that is a real triumph."

In the years that followed, some of the harsher sentiments against the Durrs—but certainly not all—softened and they were recognized for their efforts. Clifford Durr retired from the practice of

law and often delivered guest lectures at events around the country. He died in 1975.

Virginia Durr would outlive her husband by almost a quarter-century, during which time she was often honored as an important figure in the civil rights movement. She made many joint public appearances with her old friend, Rosa Parks. Her home in Montgomery continued to draw visitors, both famous and unknown, for many years. She died in 1999.

Clifford Durr traveled the country delivering lectures after the boycott until his death in 1975.
Courtesy of Walter Lyon

A Place in History

The Montgomery Bus Boycott's place in history is secure. Rosa Parks became a national icon, famous worldwide as the "Mother of the Civil Rights Movement." Montgomery, Alabama, is known officially and unofficially as the "Birthplace of the Civil Rights Movement."

But how accurate are these and similar labels? Just what were the Montgomery Bus Boycott's contributions to the civil rights movement?

There is no denying that long before Rosa Parks, Martin Luther King Jr. or even E.D. Nixon became household names, black citizens in the United States were fighting for their civil rights. The bus boycott that started in 1955 was far from the first attempt by black citizens to seek equal treatment in public transportation. Similar efforts included a boycott by blacks in Baton Rouge, Louisiana, in 1953 to push bus drivers to obey the city's ordinance permitting first-come, first-served bus seating.

The Montgomery Bus Boycott of 1955 was not even the first boycott in Montgomery designed to oppose segregated transportation seating. A short-lived boycott—like the 1955 boycott, urged by black ministers—sprang up in 1900 to protest segregated seating on the city's streetcar system. But it had no centralized organization and quickly dissipated.

Nor was the U.S. Supreme Court ruling enjoining Montgomery's segregated bus seating the first or the most important civil rights decision by the court in the 1950s. That came in May 1954, when the Supreme Court unanimously ruled in *Brown v. Board of Education of Topeka, Kansas,* that segregation in public schools was unconstitutional.

Still, the Montgomery Bus Boycott deserves its place in history as the birthplace of the modern civil rights movement for many reasons.

First and foremost, the Montgomery Bus Boycott showed the importance of having a local base when attempts were made to fight segregation. The Montgomery boycott was truly local in nature, with local leaders making all the key decisions. Certainly without the changing national legal environment reflected in key court deci-

Rosa Parks (right) waits to board a bus at the end of the Montgomery Bus Boycott on December 26, 1956.
Don Cravens/Time Life Pictures/Getty Images

Evd Bus Protest   Dec. 19
Delivered at
Holt St. Bapt.
First Bapt. Church

STATEMENT BY THE PRESIDENT OF THE MONTGOMERY IMPROVEMENT ASSOCIATION,
THE REV. M. L. KING, JR., DECEMBER 20, 1956.

For more than twelve months now, we, the Negro citizens of
Montgomery have been engaged in a non-violent protest against in-
justices and indignities experienced on city buses. We came to see
that, in the long run, it is more honorable to walk in dignity than
ride in humiliation. So in a quiet dignified manner, we decided to
substitute tired feet for tired souls, and walk the streets of
Montgomery until the sagging walls of injustice had been crushed by
the battering rams of surging justice.

Often our movement has been referred to as a boycott movement.
The word boycott, however, does not adequately describe the true
spirit of our movement. The word boycott is suggestive of merely an
economic squeeze devoid of any positive value. We have never allowed
ourselves to get bogged in the negative; we have always sought to
accentuate the positive. Our aim has never been to put the bus company
out of business, but rather to put justice in business.

These twelve months have not at all been easy. Our feet have
often been tired. We have struggle against tremendous odds to main-
tain alternative transportation. There have been moments when roaring
waters of disappointment poured upon us in staggering torrents. We
can remember days when unfavorable court decisions came upon us like
tidal waves, leaving us treading in the deep and confused waters of
despair. But amid all of this we have kept going with the faith that
as we struggle, God struggles with us, and that the arc of the moral
universe, although long, is bending toward justice. We have lived
under the agony and darkness of Good Friday with the conviction that
one day the heightening glow of Easter would emerge on the horizon.
We have seen truth crucified and goodness buried, but we have kept
going with the conviction that truth crushed to earth will rise again.

Now our faith seems to be vindicated. This morning the long
awaited mandate from the United States States Supreme Court concerning bus segregation came to Montgomery. This mandate expresses in
terms that are crystal clear that segregation in public transportation
is both legally and sociologically invalid. In the light of this
mandate and the unanimous vote rendered by the Montgomery Improvement
Association about a month ago, the year old protest against city
busses is officially called off, and the Negro citizens of Montgomery
are urged to return to the busses tomorrow morning on a non-segregated
basis.

I cannot close without giving just a word of caution. Our experience and growth during this past year of united non-violent
protest has been of such that we cannot be satisfied with a court
"victory" over our white brothers. We must respond to the decision
with an understanding of those who have oppressed us and with an
appreciation of the new adjustments that the court order poses for
them. We must be able to face up honestly to our own shortcomings.
We must act in such a way as to make possible a coming together of
white people and colored people on the basis of a real harmony of
interests and understanding. We seek an integration based on mutual
respect.

This is the time that we must evince calm dignity and wise re-
straint. Emotions must not run wild. Violence must not come from
any of us, for if we become victimized with violent intents, we will
have walked in vain, and our twelve months of glorious dignity will
be transformed into an eve of gloomy catastrophy. As we go back to
the busses let us be loving enough to turn an enemy into a friend.
We must now move from protest to reconciliation. It is my firm conviction that God is working in Montgomery. Let all men of goodwill,
both Negro and white, continue to work with Him. With this dedication we will be able to emerge from the bleak and desolate midnight
of man's inhumanity to man to the bright and glittering daybreak of
freedom and justice.

This statement from the Rev. Martin Luther King Jr. on December 20, 1956, urges the
black community to move from protest to reconciliation. *Alabama State Archives*

A group of former boycotters, including the Rev. Martin Luther King Jr. (second from left), wait at a busy bus stop following the U.S. Supreme Court ruling that segregated buses are unconstitutional.
Don Cravens/Time Life Pictures/Getty Images

sions, most notably *Brown v. Board of Education,* the Montgomery boycott likely would have achieved nothing more than a few concessions from city officials. Surely outside financial help and even outside advisers, such as Glenn Smiley of the Fellowship of Reconciliation, were crucial to the boycott's success. But that does not change the fundamental nature of the Montgomery Bus Boycott as a local movement led by the local black community itself.

The Montgomery boycott also showed the importance of the black community presenting a united front. This is not to say that frictions did not arise in the Montgomery movement; they did, and sometimes they were serious. For instance, during the midst of the boycott, a black minister who was a board member of the Montgomery Improvement Association alleged

The Rev. Ralph D. Abernathy (rear) watches young blacks taking part in an exercise to demonstrate how to show goodwill to whites on newly integrated buses.
Don Cravens/Time Life Pictures/Getty Images

for years of working for the betterment of blacks, he still had a point. Without the Montgomery Bus Boycott, King almost certainly would not have become the leading civil rights figure of the 20th Century.

One way the Montgomery Bus Boycott directly affected the Civil Rights Movement long after the boycott ended was by giving rise to the creation of the Southern Christian Leadership Conference. Under King's leadership, the SCLC supplanted the NAACP as the leading civil rights organization of the 1960s.

The Montgomery Bus Boycott also gave rise to the concept of mass nonviolent confrontation as a means of changing legal and societal norms without creating a backlash among the potentially sympathetic majority. The concept was far from new, but the Montgomery boycott showed that it could work in America. King kept it as a focus of the work of the SCLC, and it remained the primary strategy of the civil rights movement for decades.

The Montgomery Bus Boycott deserves its place in history because it was the laboratory where the strategies and tactics of the looming civil rights movement were developed and tested.

It would not have succeeded were it not for the courage and hard work of thousands of people. Some of them would become national civil rights icons, such as Rosa Parks, Martin Luther King Jr., and Ralph David Abernathy. Others would be lesser known, but still widely honored figures, such as E.D. Nixon, Fred Gray, Jo Ann Robinson, and Robert Graetz, to name a few.

But by far, the most important figures of the Montgomery Bus Boycott, the ones who made it happen, are the tens of thousands of unnamed black Montgomerians who from December 5, 1955, until December 21, 1956, walked their way to freedom.

that the group was mishandling funds. Some disagreement also arose between the ministers who led the MIA and lay leaders of the boycott over the direction it took. But for the most part, those schisms were set aside for the good of the cause or at least kept within the movement, and a united image was projected to the outside. That was a crucial reason the Montgomery Bus Boycott captured the imagination of the world.

The boycott also catapulted the Rev. Martin Luther King Jr. into the national and international spotlight. King became the face and, more importantly, the voice of the U.S. Civil Rights Movement until his assassination in 1968. E.D. Nixon often said that the focus should not be on what King did for the people of Montgomery but on what the people of Montgomery did for King. While that may have reflected Nixon's resentment later in life for his comparative lack of recognition

December 19, 1956

INTEGRATED BUS SUGGESTIONS

This is a historic week because segregation on buses has now been declared unconstitutional. Within a few days the Supreme Court Mandate will reach Montgomery and you will be re-boarding integrated buses. This places upon us all a tremendous responsibility of maintaining, in face of what could be some unpleasantness, a calm and loving dignity befitting good citizens and members of our Race. If there is violence in word or deed it must not be our people who commit it.

For your help and convenience the following suggestions are made. Will you read, study and memorize them so that our non-violent determination may not be endangered. First, some general suggestions:

1. Not all white people are opposed to integrated buses. Accept goodwill on the part of many.
2. The whole bus is now for the use of all people. Take a vacant seat.
3. Pray for guidance and commit yourself to complete non-violence in word and action as you enter the bus.
4. Demonstrate the calm dignity of our Montgomery people in your actions.
5. In all things observe ordinary rules of courtesy and good behavior.
6. Remember that this is not a victory for Negroes alone, but for all Montgomery and the South. Do not boast! Do not brag!
7. Be quiet but friendly; proud, but not arrogant; joyous, but not boistrous.
8. Be loving enough to absorb evil and understanding enough to turn an enemy into a friend.

Now for some specific suggestions:

1. The bus driver is in charge of the bus and has been instructed to obey the law. Assume that he will cooperate in helping you occupy any vacant seat.
2. Do not deliberately sit by a white person, unless there is no other seat.
3. In sitting down by a person, white or colored, say "May I" or "Pardon me" as you sit. This is a common courtesy.
4. If cursed, do not curse back. If pushed, do not push back. If struck, do not strike back, but evidence love and goodwill at all times.
5. In case of an incident, talk as little as possible, and always in a quiet tone. Do not get up from your seat! Report all serious incidents to the bus driver.
6. For the first few days try to get on the bus with a friend in whose non-violence you have confidence. You can uphold one another by a glance or a prayer.
7. If another person is being molested, do not arise to go to his defense, but pray for the oppressor and use moral and spiritual force to carry on the struggle for justice.
8. According to your own ability and personality, do not be afraid to experiment with new and creative techniques for achieving reconciliation and social change.
9. If you feel you cannot take it, walk for another week or two. We have confidence in our people. GOD BLESS YOU ALL.

THE MONTGOMERY IMPROVEMENT ASSOCIATION
THE REV. M. L. KING, JR., PRESIDENT
THE REV. W. J. POWELL, SECRETARY

This flier from the Montgomery Improvement Association contains suggestions for blacks to help make the integration of public buses as peaceful and smooth as possible. *Alabama State Archives*

The Bus Boycott Now:

MUSEUMS & SITES

Although Montgomery has changed greatly since the bus boycott days—socially and politically as well as physically—those interested in the boycott can still visit some important historic sites.

The Empire Theater, where the bus was stopped on the fateful day Rosa Parks refused to give up her seat to a white man, is no more. On that site, however, is the Rosa Parks Library and Museum. The three-story building houses the library of Troy University's Montgomery campus.

The Parks museum occupies the first floor of the building. The 7,000-square-foot interactive museum gives visitors a realistic look at Montgomery in 1955 and imparts a clear sense of the surroundings in which Mrs. Parks' historic act occurred.

Six distinct areas within the museum allow visitors to see the story of the courage of early civil rights workers. Among the exhibits are a replica of the city bus on which Mrs. Parks was sitting at the time of her arrest and a restored 1955 station wagon of the type used to provide transportation during the boycott.

The museum draws about 30,000 visitors annually.

(continued on page 133)

Tourists watch the video presentation in the bus windows at the Rosa Parks Library and Museum at Troy University in Montgomery.
Mickey Welsh/Advertiser Staff

128

ALABAMA

ROSA PARKS
MONTGOMERY BUS BOYCOTT

At the bus stop on this site on December 1, 1955, Mrs. Rosa Parks refused to give up her seat to boarding whites. This brought about her arrest, conviction, and fine. The Boycott began December 5, the day of Parks' trial, as a protest by African-Americans for unequal treatment they received on the bus line. Refusing to ride the buses, they maintained the Boycott until the U.S. Supreme Court ordered integration of public transportation one year later. Dr. Martin Luther King, Jr. led the Boycott, the beginning of the modern Civil Rights Movement.

(Continued on other side)

ALABAMA HISTORICAL ASSOCIATION

Visitors to the Rosa Parks Library and Museum, on the campus of Troy University in Montgomery, board a renovated bus on December 5, 2004. The bus has a regular route in downtown Montgomery. *Lloyd Gallman/Advertiser Staff*

Martha Flemings and her granddaughter Charese visit the bronze sculpture of Rosa Parks at the Rosa Parks Museum. *Karen S. Doerr/Advertiser Staff*

Work progresses on the Rosa Parks Museum Children's Annex in downtown Montgomery. *Lloyd Gallman/Advertiser Staff*

Johnnie Carr, president of the Montgomery Improvement Association since 1967, exits a renovated 1950s era public transit bus on December 5, 2004. The City of Montgomery unveiled the bus at the site where Rosa Parks was arrested in 1955. Behind Carr is attorney Fred Gray.

Lloyd Gallman/Advertiser Staff

A children's annex to the museum opened in late 2005. This 10,000-square-foot addition will have a more user-friendly approach to telling the story of the bus boycott. A "time machine bus" will transport children through time and illustrate history from the 1800s to the present. The annex will also include information on some of the less well-known people who were part of the boycott.

The Rosa Parks Library and Museum is at 251 Montgomery Street. Tours may be arranged by calling (334) 241-8616.

More information about the museum is available online at http://montgomery.troy.edu/museum/.

Martin Luther King Jr. would become the nation's leading civil rights figure and the winner of the Nobel Peace Prize. His rise to fame began

ALABAMA

DEXTER AVENUE KING MEMORIAL
BAPTIST CHURCH

Organized 1877

The second black Baptist Church in Montgomery.
First pastor was Rev. C. O. Boothe. Present
structure built 1885. Designed by Pelham J.
Anderson; built by William Watkins, a member
of the congregation.

Many prominent black citizens of Montgomery
have been members. Rev. Martin Luther King, Jr.
served as pastor (1954-1960). Montgomery bus
boycott organized here December 2, 1955.

ALABAMA HISTORICAL ASSOCIATION   1980

in Montgomery when the young minister was chosen as the public leader of the boycott. King was pastor of Dexter Avenue Baptist Church from 1954-60.

After his death, the church was renamed Dexter Avenue King Memorial Baptist Church and continues to bear that name today.

There are guided tours of the historic church, at 454 Dexter Avenue.

Tours may be booked via e-mail at tours@dexterkingmemorial.org. The church's telephone number is (334) 263-3970

While King was pastor at Dexter Avenue, he and his family lived in the church's parsonage at 309 South Jackson Street. The house was bombed during the boycott. The explosion from a bomb placed on the porch damaged the front of the house, but did not injure Mrs. King, their young daughter or a church member visiting at the time. King was not at home when the attack occurred, but came to the house shortly afterward and managed to calm an angry crowd that wanted to retaliate with violence.

The parsonage has been restored, along with the furnishings used during the King family's time there, and is now a museum open for viewing.

The telephone number is (334) 261-3270.

Holt Street Baptist Church is another boycott-era landmark. The church, at 903 South Holt Street, was the site of important mass meetings before and during the boycott. Tours of the church may be arranged by appointment by calling (334) 263-0522.

For years before the boycott, E.D. Nixon had been a respected leader in Montgomery's black community. Although he was sometimes called the father of the bus boycott, Nixon's behind-the-scenes contributions and organizational skills were not always properly recognized.

There is a historic marker in front of Nixon's former home at 647 Clinton Street.

Nixon also donated his papers to Alabama State University, which still houses the collection. They can be seen by appointment.

Although it is not located in Montgomery, the Rosa and Raymond Parks Institute for Self-Development often draws interest from persons studying the history of the boycott. The institute in Detroit, Michigan, Rosa Parks's home for many years after she left Montgomery, conducts a variety of educational programs.

More information on the institute may be obtained by calling (313) 965-1918 or sending e-mail to general@rosaparks.org.

The King Center in Atlanta, Georgia, was established in 1968 after the assassination of the civil rights leader. His widow, Coretta Scott King, was the founder and longtime chief executive officer of the center.

Located within the Martin Luther King Jr. National Historic Site in King's hometown, the center houses King's tomb, a library and archives, and various forms of media used to educate visitors about King's life and philosophy of nonviolence.

The King Center is at 449 Auburn Avenue NE in Atlanta. The telephone number is (404) 526-8900. The e-mail address for general information is information@thekingcenter.org.

A plaque in front directs visitors to Dexter Avenue King Memorial Baptist Church, where Martin Luther King Jr. was once pastor. *Mickey Welsh/Advertiser Staff*

Rosa Parks sits in front of the civil rights mural at the Dexter Avenue King Memorial Baptist Church on November 21, 1991. Parks was at the church for a Montgomery Improvement Association meeting.
Mickey Welsh/Advertiser Staff

Further Reading

Before Brown: Civil Rights and White Backlash in the Modern South. Edited by Glenn Feldman. University of Alabama Press, 2004.

Bus Ride to Justice: Changing the System by the System; The Life and Works of Fred Gray. Fred Gray. New South Books, 2002.

Daybreak of Freedom: The Montgomery Bus Boycott. Edited by Stewart Burns. University of North Carolina Press, 1997.

Dividing Lines: Municipal Politics and the Struggle for Civil Rights in Montgomery, Birmingham, and Selma. J. Mills Thornton III. University of Alabama Press, 2002.

Freedom Writer: Virginia Foster Durr, Letters from the Civil Rights Years. Edited by Patricia Sullivan. Routledge, 2003.

The Montgomery Bus Boycott and the Women Who Started It: The Memoir of Jo Ann Gibson Robinson. Edited by David J. Garrow. University of Tennessee Press, 1987.

Rosa Parks. Douglas Brinkley. Viking, 2000.

The Walking City: The Montgomery Bus Boycott, 1955-1956. Edited by David J. Garrow. Carlson Publishing, 1989.

When the Church Bell Rang Racist: The Methodist Church and the Civil Rights Movement in Alabama. Donald E. Collins. Mercer University Press, 1998.

A White Preacher's Memoir: The Montgomery Bus Boycott. Robert S. Graetz. Black Belt Press, 1999.